The Desert Smells Like Rain

T0154964

THE DESERT SMELLS LIKE
RAIN

A Naturalist in O'odham Country

Gary Paul Nabhan

**THE UNIVERSITY OF
ARIZONA PRESS**

TUCSON

Since the publication of this edition in 1982, the Papago Indian Tribe has officially changed its name to Tohono O'odham (Desert People). This change became effective with the adoption of the new constitution in January 1986 by members of the Tohono O'odham Nation.

The University of Arizona Press
www.uapress.arizona.edu

We respectfully acknowledge the University of Arizona is on the land and territories of Indigenous peoples. Today, Arizona is home to twenty-two federally recognized tribes, with Tucson being home to the O'odham and the Yaqui. Committed to diversity and inclusion, the University strives to build sustainable relationships with sovereign Native Nations and Indigenous communities through education offerings, partnerships, and community service.

This edition is published by arrangement with North Point Press, a division of Farrar, Straus and Giroux, LLC.
First University of Arizona Press paperbound edition 2002
40th anniversary edition published 2022

ISBN-13: 978-0-8165-4689-3 (paperback)
ISBN-13: 978-0-8165-4861-3 (ebook)

Cover design by Leigh McDonald
Cover art by Michael Chiago Sr.
Typeset by Sara Thaxton in 12/15 Adobe Text Pro with Kinesis Std

The author would like to thank *Planet Drum, La Confiuencia: A Magazine for the Southwest, Sun Tracks*, and *Dry Country News*, who first published portions of this text.

The photographs on pages 4, 29, 82, 126, copyright 1982 by C. Allan Morgan. The photographs on pages 54, 62, 92, 104, printed courtesy of Arizona State Museum, University of Arizona. The photographs on pages 18, 44, 70, copyright 1982 by Gary Paul Nabhan.

The Library of Congress Cataloging-in-Publication has cataloged the first University of Arizona Press paperbound edition as
Nabhan, Gary Paul.
The desert smells like rain : a naturalist in O'odham country / Gary Paul Nabhan
p. cm.
Originally published : The desert smells like rain: a naturalist in Papago country.
San Francisco : North Point Press, © 1982.
Includes bibliographical references.
ISBN 978-0-8165-2249-1 (paper: alk. paper)
1. Tohono O'odham Indians. 2. Indigenous peoples—Ecology—Sonoran Desert. 3. Desert ecology—Sonoran Desert. 4. Natural history—Sonoran Desert. 5. Sonoran Desert—Environmental conditions. I. Title.
E99.P25.N32   2002
970.3.PI97N   2002   2002018732

Printed in the United States of America
♾ This paper meets the requirements of ANSI/NISO Z39.48-1992 (Permanence of Paper).

This book is in thanks to the *Ge Hemajkam* of the Desert People.

Contents

Preface to the 40th Anniversary Edition

As I write this in the summer of 2021, communities in southern Arizona and northern Sonora have received four to five times more precipitation than they had in the previous year. Suddenly, I hear individuals of all cultures and walks of life saying a phrase that echoed something an eight-year-old Tohono O'odham boy said to me in the late 1970s:

"The desert smells like rain again."

The monsoons had brought the Sonoran Desert enough moisture that the soil's banks of dormant seeds sprouted, flowered, and fruited, reproducing prolifically. All manner of edible and medicinal plants appeared for the first time in years. Some thirteen highly aromatic volatile oils—emitted by a dozen and a half Sonoran Desert plants, not just creosote—filled the air with fragrances that we had not smelled for many moons and seasons.

I am one of many who felt *gratitude*—to our Creator and to the desert itself—for reminding us of the hidden abundance held within arid landscapes. But I also felt a deep gratitude to the Tohono O'odham and Hia ch-eḍ O'odham individuals and communities of the Sonoran Desert who first introduced me to this hidden abundance nearly half a century ago. With patience, cross-cultural tolerance, intelligence, and soulfulness, several dozen O'odham elders, adolescents, and contemporaries offered me a fleeting glimpse of their world—their cosmovision, or *O'odham himdag*. They forever changed the way I looked at, smelled, and savored life on "Planet Desert"—this place that all of us call home.

All of my early encounters with the O'odham now seem to me to be rather fortuitous; that is, they were not anything I could have earned, deserved, or planned for. Instead, they came upon me as suddenly as a summer thunderstorm, humbling me with their generosity, spirituality, and grace. I did not originally come to what the historians call Papagueria—*O'odham ha-jewed*—to "study" another culture, nor to "missionize" anyone to my ways of thinking or doing.

Instead, I came as an Arab American whose grandparents had left another desert halfway around the world—as refugees from war, locust plagues, and water scarcity. My father, my grandfathers, and many of my aunts and uncles who knew "our" arid-adapted traditions had recently passed; I was left heartbroken, scared, rudderless, and adrift in a desert as large as an ocean, detached from my own roots. I was also broke—not just broken—and was looking for work "outside" that would reconnect me with both desert nature and the many cultures that were rooted in those landscapes of solitude and silence, sand and wind.

Somehow, I was accepted to the Arizona "Writers on the Road" program, which placed poets and novelists in grade schools and junior highs to teach writing to minority youth. By luck, I was placed in Tohono O'odham, Pima, and Hopi schools for brief stints of teaching schoolchildren about how to write, even as they taught me about their homelands. Soon, I was visiting farmers and foragers after school to learn about what and how they planted to successfully farm in a land so dry that few others could make ends meet under such daunting conditions. I pitched in, lending a hand wherever I could.

And then a nonprofit nutrition and gardening program that trained Tohono O'odham community health representatives and assisted farmers offered me a field job. Each morning at 6 a.m., I would head out from Tucson to the Rez to help elderly farmers plant, fertilize, or harvest their fields; to give bilingual workshops on healthy foods and beverages; or to lend a hand at festivals and fairs. In short, I was in service to families and communities who requested technical food and farming assistance, but in no way was I an agronomic expert or an ethnographer. I simply offered my hands and heart to any O'odham family that requested help. I was not there to survey them but to accompany them in meeting needs that they themselves defined. And if I was involved in plowing with draft animals, sowing, harvesting, praying, and observing a baptism, seasonal rite, or ceremony, it was because someone in the community quietly invited me to stay around a little longer. Later, as my own nomadic life settled down some, I was able to offer room in my own home, as well as food and beds, to several O'odham youth and elders who then became part of my own extended family.

At first, I kept no journal or diary, but then, as the power of what elders were telling me and youth were alerting me to sunk in, I realized that I needed to record their words and their traditional knowledge so that I could more deeply reflect and meditate on what I was learning—it was a kind of vernacular knowledge that I had only known from my grandpa, Ferhat Nabhan, who had shared with me from his years as a fruit peddler and shepherd, before he had to flee as a refugee from the deserts of the Middle East. Here I was—along another border in the desert— where families had been fragmented and disrupted by an artificial line drawn in the sand. It dawned on me that the insults and humilities that the O'odham had suffered at the hands of both Mexican and U.S. federal workers were much like those my own

Arab cousins still suffer near the borders of Lebanon, Syria, and Israel. I listened keenly to learn how they had dealt with countless invasions and potential conflicts with such strength, resilience, and spiritual depth.

It was then that I realized that the O'odham were not merely teaching me how to farm but how to live with faith, integrity, and self-determination in such a conflicted world. After being patiently tutored in the *O'odham ha-neoki* dialects by Ofelia Zepeda, Tony Chana, Danny Lopez, Ken Hale, Jane Hill, Sally Pablo, Ruth Giff, Ramona Mattias, Culver Cassa, and Phillip Salcido, I came to understand how richly nuanced their expressions for daily life in the desert really were. To put it bluntly, they are the true experts on O'odham language and culture, and I do not, cannot, nor will not ever claim such status.

Looking back at the writing of a twenty-five- to twenty-nine-year-old "greenhorn" from over four decades ago for the first time in many years, I can now spot passages that seem presumptuous or overly romantic, off-the-mark or somewhat intrusive. For that, I ask for forgiveness from the families of the elders who offered me their wisest and more thoughtful explanations of how the world works or, at least, how it should work. But what matters most in this little book is their words, not mine.

Let me give you just one example of a "prophesy" hidden in the text that has haunted me to this very day. A shy but eloquent elder named Jerome Ascencio alerted me to the possibility that "the rains were dying" and that *ak-chin* floodwater farming, an ancient form of water harvesting to grow and irrigate food crops, would not survive much longer. I could see in his fields and in his oral histories the changing frequencies of drought years and abundant harvests that there was validity to his concerns. But when I went into the offices of university and federal agency climatologists in the early 1980s to see if they could verify or confirm that precipitation patterns were shifting on the Tohono O'odham Reservation or Sonoran Desert at large, they dismissed the possibility that long-term climate change was affecting any Arizona farmers.

"Look at how few annual rainfall records have been kept out on the reservation. . . . We can't prove anything with such a small data set."

"Are you sure that its not climate shifts but human impacts of livestock grazing or building cattle tanks that has diminished the volume of runoff that reaches their fields?"

"A lot of old farmers are superstitious and don't accurately remember how much rain fell when they were young. . . . They just glorify the old days."

Today, we can conclude that Jerome Ascencio and many other O'odham farmers had correctly observed that the timing and intensity of summer rainfall and runoff events were already shifting in a manner that would sooner or later affect their farming traditions. Climate change is not a fantasy, and it has taken us into a "new normal." And since Jerome candidly expressed to me his concern about changing patterns of summer rains, those trends have been scientifically confirmed. More than 90 percent of the floodwater-fed acreage of crops grown then has since atrophied on Tohono O'odham Nation lands. The fields lie abandoned—in waiting—hoping for better days.

And so, many of the lucid observations of the O'odham whom I quoted in that little book (that Wendell Berry edited for me in 1981) have even greater cultural significance today than in those yesteryears. Those include the O'odham elders' perception that their native desert foods formerly protected their ancestors from diabetes and other infirmities, a "hypothesis" that epidemiologists, nutrition educators, and dieticians dismissed in the 1970s, but that evidence from several different kinds of studies bear out. Today many programs on reservations are judiciously and effectively using desert foods and Indigenous knowledge on how to prepare them in health promotion.

Delores Lewis's concerns about biodiversity declines at desert oases once managed by the O'odham as sacred places "where the birds were our friends" also seem prophetic. At the Quitobaquito Springs on the Arizona-Sonora border, where irrigated orchards once extended to both sides of the border, historic orchards are no longer irrigated by National Park Service resource managers; all the fruit trees are now dead. The largest shift in the avifauna of this oasis appeared to have occurred just after 1956, when the Park Service illegally evicted all O'odham residents from the area, "buying" title to this ancient settlement by providing a one-time cash payment to a single descendant for the only artesian-fed springs for twenty miles in any direction.

Moreover, during the year and a half period in 2019–2020 when the thirty-foot-tall border wall was being built across the southern edges of Organ Pipe Cactus Monument, heavy equipment traffic, aquifer mining, dynamiting, dust, and other disruptions radically reduced water availability and birdlife at the historic oasis. While forty-seven bird species—including many swimming birds—were not observed at the oasis during the construction period, twelve mudflat birds arrived to forage in the area surrounding the drastically diminished pond. O'odham prayers and protests did not dissuade the Army Corps of Engineers from wreaking havoc on a sacred site in a wilderness area within a UNESCO Biophere Reserve, but hundreds of thousands of Americans expressed their support for continued O'odham access to the site.

Over the long haul, though, O'odham prayers, actions, and knowledge of sacred waters in the desert may hold sway. For the first time in U.S. history, 2021 ushered in the first Native American secretary of interior and the first Native American to serve as the director of the National Park Service.

I mention these two instances where traditional O'odham knowledge has been found to hold scientific validity not because Native knowledge of the natural world and Western scientific knowledge are mirror images of one another. In fact, I would argue that the O'odham way of integrating precise observations, cultural values, and ethics is in many ways superior to Western science, which frequently falls into a reductionistic, amoral stance.

But over the last two years of rekindling friendships with Tohono O'odham and Hia ch-eḍ O'odham political and spiritual leaders and educators as we have worked together on issues as diverse as COVID-19 prevention, social justice for transborder tribes, sacred personhood for saguaros, and constitutionally guaranteed freedom of spiritual expression, I remain amazed at the intelligence, wisdom, compassion, and ethical integrity still embedded in O'odham communities on both sides of the border. And I remain humbled by the good will and humor that many families have offered me over the decades.

Like my unending awe and gratitude for each rain that blesses us here on Planet Desert, I remain in awe of the distinctiveness and dignity of O'odham culture, and grateful for its continued presence among us. O'odham writers and storytellers such as Ofelia Zepeda, Camillus Lopez, Frances Manual, Laura Kerman, Juanita Ahill, Lorraine Eiler, Danny Lopez, Michael Chiago Sr., Leonard Chana, Barnaby Lewis, and others too numerous to name have already excelled at telling their own stories from the *inside*. Indeed, most of these artists and scholars have also been generous enough to share those stories with those of us from other cultural traditions. I also look forward to seeing, hearing, or reading more of the expressions of the many fine up-and-coming O'odham poets, singers, novelists, filmmakers, and storytellers whose images, values, and visions will far outstrip any skewed views that you can garner from this little rainfed field of dreams.

Acknowledgments

Decades ago, a Sonoran told explorer Carl Lumholtz that "to arrive at a Papago house is like coming to one's relatives." I'm grateful for such Papago friends who have taken me in, sharing their homes, hearts, work, food, and goodness with me. At times it is like being with my own Lebanese aunts and uncles.

For this reason, I wish to thank whole families, rather than single out any individuals: the Lewises, the Ascencios, the Enriquezes, the Ahills, the Valenzuelas, the Pablos, the Lopezes, the Garcias, the Antones, the Williamses, the Noriegos, the Xaviers, the Maristos, the Mattias, the Zepedas, and the Channas.

Yet these friends are not the characters named in this book. The fictitious Papago in the chapters which follow are composites of several people—a character is not intended to represent a particular real-life person. I've used this poetic license for two reasons. Individuals deserve privacy, and the *O'odham Himdag*, the Papago Way, is more encompassing than any one person's knowledge. My friends generally prefer not to be singled out as "native experts." Likewise, I can neither "possess" the desert, nor the knowledge they have shared. And despite the help of many Papago, nothing here is meant to convey an "official" Papago viewpoint.

Some non-Papago have aided in these journeys into the desert, and I have learned from them too: Karen Reichhardt, an observant plant ecologist; Cynthia Anson, an applied anthropologist with many insights; and Amadeo Rea, an ethnobiologist, who first introduced me to O'odham families. A number of other friends have joined us on field trips as well: Tom, Muffin, Jan, Steve, Kit, Nancy, Peter, Brian, Russ, Dennis, Will, Wade, Chuck, and Jim. Henry Dobyns and Bunny Fontana have helped shape my thoughts on Papago history, as has Richard Felger on ethnobiology. Sally Pablo, Father Richard, Sister Dorothy, and Sister Ann always kept their doors open for me. Carri Niethammer, Mahina Drees, Wendell Berry, and Ann Zwinger gave me the encouragement needed to complete the book. I'm grateful for the talents of Helga Teiwes and Al Morgan, photographers, and Jack Shoemaker, a thoughtful and gracious editor. Bless you all. Bless the desert.

Gary Paul Nabhan
San Ignacio, Sonora

O'odham Sounds
Symbols and Pronunciation,
Alvarez and Hale Orthography

Symbols used here	Approximate English equivalent	Papago Example	(meaning)
a	p*o*t	'*a*li	(children)
b	*b*ear	*b*an	(coyote)
c	*ch*ile	cu*c*ul	(chicken)
d	bu*d*	ñei*d*	(to see)
ḍ	bu*tt*er	me*ḍ*	(to run)
e	p*u*t (or German ü)	'*e*ṣa	(to plant)
g	*g*oose	*g*o*g*s	(dog)
h	*h*air	*h*a:l	(squash)
i	*e*vent	'*i*:wakĭ	(greens)
ĭ	unvoiced i, at end of word	'i:wak*ĭ*	(greens)
j	*j*udge	*j*eweḍ	(earth)
k	*k*ick	*k*awiyu	(horse)
l	Spanish trilled l/r	*l*anjekĭ	(lentils)
m	*m*oon	*m*ansa:na	(apple)
n	*n*ose	*n*alaṣ	(orange)

ñ	pi*ny*on, pi*ñ*on	*ñ*eid	(to see)
o	b*o*at, rarely *aw*l	'*o*las	(round)
p	*p*addle	*p*an	(bread)
s	*s*ick	mi:*s*a	(table)
ş	*sh*ovel	*ş*awoñ	(soap)
t	*t*urtle	*t*obĭ	(bunny)
u	b*oo*t	m*u*:la	(mule)
w	*w*alk	*w*atto	(ramada)
	(or sloughed-off *v*)		
'	glottal stop	'*a*'al	(children)

A long, even vowel is represented by the vowel symbol followed by a colon—as in *mu:la*.

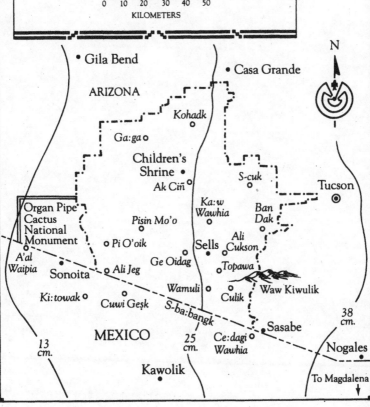

PAPAGO INDIAN COUNTRY

$^{13}_{cm.}$ *Rainfall in Centimeters*

• *Major Towns in Papago Country*

○ *Traditional Papago Villages with Fields Nearby*

SCALE

0   10 20 30 40 50

KILOMETERS

N

• Gila Bend

• Casa Grande

ARIZONA

Kohadk ○

Ga:ga ○

Children's
Shrine •

Ak Ciñ ○

S-cuk ○

Tucson ◉

*Ka:w
Wawhia*

*Ban
Dak*

Organ Pipe
Cactus
National
Monument ○

Pisin Mo'o ○

○ *Pi O'oik*

*Ali
Cukson* ○

Sells •

A'al
Waipia ○

Sonoita

○ *Ali Jeg*

Ge Oidag ○

Topawa ○

Waw Kiwulik

Ki:towak ○

○
Cuwi Geşk

Wamuli ○

S-ba:bangk

Culik ○

38
cm.

13
cm.

MEXICO

25
cm.

*Ce:dagi
Wawhia* ○

• Sasabe

Nogales
•

Kawolik
•

To Magdalena
↓

Let me say this before rain becomes a utility that they can plan and distribute for money. By 'they' I mean the people who cannot understand that rain is a festival. The time will come when they will sell you even your rain.

THOMAS MERTON

An Overture

With many dust storms, with many lightnings, with many
thunders, with many rainbows, it started to go.
From within wet mountains, more clouds came out and
joined it.

JOSEPH PANCHO, *MOCKINGBIRD SPEECH*

Last Saturday before dusk, the summer's 114-degree heat broke to 79 within an hour. A fury of wind whipped up, pelting houses with dust, debris, and gravel. Then a scatter of rain came, as a froth of purplish clouds charged across the skies. As the last of the sun's light dissipated, we could see Baboquivari Peak silhouetted on a red horizon, lightning dancing around its head.

The rains came that night—they changed the world.

Crusty dry since April, the desert floor softened under the rain's dance. Near the rain-pocked surface, hundreds of thousands of wild sprouts of bloodroot amaranth are popping off their seedcoats and diving toward light. Barren places will soon be shrouded in a veil of green.

Desert arroyos are running again, muddy water swirling after a head of suds, dung, and detritus. Where sheetfloods pool, buried animals awake, or new broods hatch. At dawn, dark egg-shaped clouds of flying ants hover over ground, excited in the early morning light.

In newly filled waterholes, spadefoot toads suddenly congre-

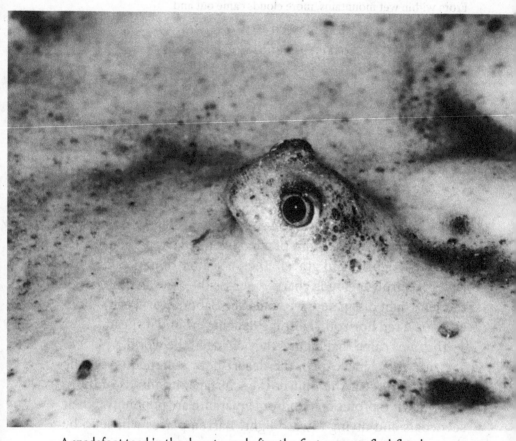
A spadefoot toad in the desert pond after the first summer flashflood.

gate. The males bellow. They seek out mates, then latch onto them with their special nuptial pads. The females spew out egg masses into the hot murky water. For two nights, the toad ponds are wild with chanting while the Western spadefoot's burnt-peanut-like smell looms thick in the air.

A yellow mud turtle crawls out of the drenched bottom of an old adobe borrow pit where he had been buried through the hot dry spell. He plods a hundred yards over to a floodwater reservoir and dives in. He has no memory of how many days it's been since his last swim, but the pull of the water—*that* is somehow familiar.

This is the time when the Papago Indians of the Sonoran Desert celebrate the coming of the rainy season moons, the *Jujkiabig Mamṣad,* and the beginning of a new year.

Fields lying fallow since the harvest of the winter crop are now ready for another planting. If sown within a month after summer solstice, they can produce a crop quick enough for harvest by the Feast of San Francisco, October 4.

When I went by the Madrugada home in Little Tucson on Monday, the family was eagerly talking about planting the flash-flood field again. At the end of June, Julian wasn't even sure if he would plant this year—no rain yet, too hot to prepare the field, and hardly any water left in their *charco* catchment basin.

Now, a fortnight later, the pond is nearly filled up to the brim. Runoff has fed into it through four small washes. Sheetfloods have swept across the field surface. Julian imagines big yellow squash blossoms in his field, just another month or so away. It makes his mouth water.

Once I asked a Papago youngster what the desert smelled like to him. He answered with little hesitation:

"The desert smells like rain."

His reply is a contradiction in the minds of most people. How could the desert smell like rain, when deserts are, by definition, places which lack substantial rainfall?

The boy's response was a sort of Papago shorthand. Hearing Papago can be like tasting a delicious fruit, while sensing that the taste comes from a tree with roots too deep to fathom.

The question had triggered a scent—creosote bushes after a storm—their aromatic oils released by the rains. His nose remembered being out in the desert, overtaken: *the desert smells like rain.*

Most outsiders are struck by the apparent absence of rain in deserts, feeling that such places lack something vital. Papago, on the other hand, are intrigued by the unpredictability rather than the paucity of rainfall—theirs is a dynamic, lively world, responsive to stormy forces that may come at any time.

A Sonoran Desert village may receive five inches of rain one year and fifteen the next. A single storm may dump an inch and a half in the matter of an hour on one field and entirely skip another a few miles away. Dry spells lasting four months may be broken by a single torrential cloudburst, then resume again for several more months. Unseasonal storms, and droughts during the customary rainy seasons, are frequent enough to reduce patterns to chaos.

The Papago have become so finely tuned to this unpredictability that it shapes the way they speak of rain. It has also ingrained itself deeply in the structure of their language.

Linguist William Pilcher has observed that the Papago discuss events in terms of their probability of occurrence, avoiding any assumption that an event will happen for sure:

> . . . it is my impression that the Papago abhor the idea of making definite statements. I am still in doubt as to how close a rain storm must be before one may properly say *t'o tju:* (It is going to rain on us), rather than *tki 'o tju:ks* (something like: It looks like it may be going to rain on us).

Since few Papago are willing to confirm that something will happen until it does, an element of surprise becomes part of almost everything. Nothing is ever really cut and dried. When rains do come, they're a gift, a windfall, a lucky break.

Elderly Papago have explained to me that rain is more than just water. There are different ways that water comes to living things, and what it brings with it affects how things grow.

Remedio Cruz was once explaining to me why he plants the old White Sonora variety of wheat when he does. He had waited for some early January rains to gently moisten his field before he planted.

"That Pap'go wheat—it's good to plant just in January or early February. It grows good on just the rainwater from the sky. It would not do good with water from the *ground*, so that's why we plant it when those soft winter rains come to take care of it."

In the late 1950s, a Sonoran Desert ecologist tried to simulate the gentle winter rains in an attempt to make the desert bloom. Lloyd Tevis used untreated groundwater from a well, sprayed up through a sprinkler, to encourage wildflower germination on an apparently lifeless patch of desert. While Tevis did trigger germination of one kind of desert wildflower with a little less than two inches of fake rain, none germinated with less than an inch. In general, production of other wildflowers required more than three or four inches of fake rain.

Tevis was then surprised to see what happened when less than an inch of real rain fell on his experimental site in January. He noticed in the previously sparse vegetation "a tremendous emergence of seedlings. Real rain demonstrated an extraordinary superiority over the artificial variety to bring about a high rate of germination." With one particular kind of desert wildflower, seedlings were fifty-six times more numerous after nearly an inch of real rain than they were after the more intense artificial watering.

The stimulating power of rain in the desert is simply more than moisture. Be it the nutrients released in a rainstorm, or the physical force of the water, there are other releasing mechanisms associated with rainwater. But even if someone worked up a better simulation of rain using *fortified* groundwater, would it be very useful in making the desert bloom?

Doubtful. Remedio himself wonders about the value of ground water pumping for farming, for water is something he *sings* rather than pumps into his field. Every summer, Remedio and a few elderly companions sing to bring the waters from the earth and sky to meet each other. Remedio senses that only with this meeting will his summer beans, corn, and squash grow. A field relying solely on groundwater would not have what it takes. He has heard that well water has some kind of "medicine" (chemical) in it that is no good for crops. In addition, he believes that groundwater pumping as much as twenty miles away adversely affects the availability of moisture to his field.

I joined in a study with other scientists to compare the nutritive value of tepary beans grown in Papago flashflood fields with those grown in modern Anglo-American-style groundwater-irrigated fields nearby. The protein content of the teparies grown in the traditional flashflood environments tended to be higher than that of the same tepary bean varieties grown with water pumped from the ground. Production appeared to be more efficient in the Papago fields—more food energy was gained with less energy in labor and fuel spent. No wonder—it is a way of agriculture that has fine-tuned itself to local conditions over generations.

There they are, Julian and Remedio—growing food in a desert too harsh for most kinds of agriculture—using cues that few of us would ever notice. Their sense of how the desert works comes from decades of day-to-day observations. These perceptions have been filtered through a cultural tradition that has been refined, honed, and handed down over centuries of living in arid places.

If others wish to adapt to the Sonoran Desert's peculiarities, this ancient knowledge can serve as a guide. Yet the best guide will tell you: there are certain things you must learn on your own. The desert is unpredictable, enigmatic. One minute you will be smelling dust. The next, the desert can smell just like rain.

CHAPTER 1

On the Trail of I'itoi

A Pilgrimage into the Baboquivari Mountains

An earth crack;
an earth crack!
Out of it I'itoi comes.
To the sky he takes me. . . .

SONG DREAMED BY A PAPAGO SHAMAN

We felt watched from the time we began our pilgrimage, one crisp November morning at *Ali Cukṣon*, Arizona. That is, Little Tucson, a Papago Indian village five-hundredths the size of and fifty miles southwest of its burgeoning counterpart. While metropolitan Tucson is the largest city in the U.S. based solely on groundwater resources, *Ali Cukṣon* is the home of desert Indians who distrust the medicine taste of well water, preferring to grow their modest gardens with the runoff provided by sporadic rains.

So from the start, as a caracara swept above our pickup, trailing down the road with us a while, we felt watched. Not by spectators, spies, or spooks, but by sentient beings. The caracara was just one of our guides along the way, yet it exemplified the rare nature of the biotic community through which we were journeying. The caracara does not nest in too many places north of Mexico, but it does so as a permanent resident near *Ali Cukṣon*. Caracaras and two other carrion-eaters, black and turkey vultures, thrive here on the western rim of the Baboquivari Mountains, beyond modern agriculture's assault on the desert with pump and pesticides. Our journey that day was into the midst of the Babo-quivaris, to a place so sacred for the Papago that it has been designated as a tribal shrine, a natural/spiritual sanctuary.

The place is a cave hidden at the base of the cliffs which form the walls of Baboquivari Canyon. It is *I'itoi Ki:*, the home of the Coyote-like character responsible for the Papago emergence into this world. After creating humans, deer, fire, bald-headed buzzards, and much mischief, *I'itoi* settled down to spend the rest of his existence underground. *I'itoi* only occasionally comes out of his sanctuary these days—for instance, he helped guide wildlife to safety when the first locomotive roared through Papago Country. Now, the Desert People mostly visit the cave knowing that he is out of sight, but nevertheless watching them, granting children luck, and providing medicine men with the healing power they request.

The cave, in legend, is an antechamber of a large labyrinth winding within the Baboquivaris. Papago basketmakers weave a design to signify this—a small man standing at the beginning of a circular maze. This design, also known as *I'itoi Ki:*, is allegorical, too—they say it is the Papago searching for the deeper meaning of life. The real cave is still a spiritual touchstone for these Desert People today. Because Baboquivari Peak towering over the cave can be seen from nearly every village on the reservation, this place is literally and figuratively at the heart of the Papago universe.

Our truckload of Papago and Anglos was driven by many de-sires—to ask *I'itoi* for blessings, to feel the excitement of searching for a place we had all heard of many times, and to be in the beauty of a canyon known for its wildlife and strange plants. With a special permit on the dashboard, we turned off the paved road to Topawa and headed thirteen miles east through the restricted-access range of the Papago Reservation. Salvador, still celebrating from the night before, passionately sang Papago songs "handed down from *I'itoi*" as the dust cloud flowed in around us in the back of the pickup. High above the peak, a soaring Harris' hawk watched a white streak of dust stir up and lengthen toward the canyon. A bobcat stood in the road for a moment, puzzling at the pickup looming larger and larger, then bounded away into the brush.

We reached the road's end where an old stone cabin and a floodwater field stood abandoned. There was something tropical about the canyon at this point—the northernmost remnants of thornscrub vegetation characteristic of western Mexico. Among the creekside desert olives, mesquite, catclaw, and hackberries, some tropical elements crop up: kidneywood, Arizona sapote, white flowered plumbago, bloodleaf amaranth, and wild chile bushes. There are other, rarer plants—desert dogbane and an elephant tree—that are only known in the U.S. on the western edge of the Baboquivaris. The canyon is one of the few localities in the U.S. where five-striped sparrows nest, and that the raccoon-like coatimundis frequent. These relic plant and animal populations persist in the midst of an other-worldly landscape: volcanic outcrops studded with giant cactus.

As we piled out of the truck, Salvador and his seventy-four-year-old mother, Mona, anxiously pointed towards the base of the cliffs hundreds of feet above us. In their native language, they discussed the landmarks that would guide us to the cave—the color and pattern of weathering on the rock just above it, the zigzag that the trail was supposed to take, and the direction that the cave was said to face. Neither of them had been to the cave before, although the many descriptions heard around lifetimes of campfires had impressed images in their minds.

Yet, both knew the canyon well. Mona had camped on its edge with her family more than half a century before, when they would gather cactus fruit on the surrounding slopes. She remembered that one of her cousins, while out hunting javelina for meat for the camp, had come upon some ancient ruins on the top of an adjacent mesa at dusk. Among them, he found several intact pottery vessels, which he brought back down to the makeshift ramada shelters under which the family slept.

Suddenly, a wind whipped up out of the canyon and roared through the camp, knocking down the ramada where the stolen pottery stood. The young man's family made him take the vessels back where they belonged, and Mona has since maintained a fear of disturbing "the gone ones."

When younger, Salvador had hunted in the area with an uncle who spent years prior to that as the only big-game hunter in their village. Not everyone was allowed to hunt, and those who did observed strict taboos, and lived like ascetics for weeks at a time while on the stalk. Salvador had also gathered wild chiles, onions, and edible roots in the higher elevations of the Baboquivaris.

Now, however, Mona was too old and Salvador was too hung over to join us; Baptisto, his younger brother, would guide us up. Salvador repeated all he remembered of descriptions of where the cave should be, and left us, saying, "I will sing for *I'itoi* to make you a path."

As Salvador resigned himself to staying, Mona became apprehensive about my wife Karen and me.

"You can't just go in there, you know, you got to leave him any little thing. When you go into the cave you just give whatever you have—a penny, a hair barrette, a cigarette.

"There was a Catholic Sister who took some Papago boys up there. She went in with them, but she didn't give anything, thinking that nothing would happen because she was a Sister.

"Then the boys who had each left something went back out and she turned around to go too. But it looked all dark and where she came in just kept getting smaller and smaller until she couldn't fit through. Then the boys yelled 'Give something, Sister!' and she finally left her rosary beads so it would open just enough to let her get out of there."

"Don't worry, Mona," my wife interjected. "We'll give what

we have and leave something for you too so he'll know you're down here."

"Oh really? That sure would be good!"

Baptisto, Karen, and I started up the canyon on a trail through the dense riparian undergrowth. At one point, I came to an opening just as two white-tailed deer exploded into the brush on the other side, driving uphill over a knoll and out of sight.

I'itoi had made the first deer by overstuffing a desert mouse, leaving the white stuffing showing on the belly underneath. As I saw the last flap of the white tails dip over the knoll, I guessed that we had come across *I'itoi's* own privately run herd.

The flight of the deer caused a ruckus in the brush, with Mexican jays, Gambel's quail, cactus wrens, and phainopeplas noisily fleeing, too. Judging from the indignant voices, I felt as though we had busted up some kind of illicit activity hidden in the dense thicket.

This far up the canyon, we saw Mexican blue oak, mulberry, and huge jojoba, thriving in the more humid narrows of the canyons. Here, we encountered potholes full of standing water along the otherwise dry creekbed. The red flowers of desert honeysuckle and hummingbird-trumpet still brightened the way this late in the fall.

Baptisto guessed that we should make a turn away from the creekbed and begin our way up the steep scree of the slope. We left the musky shade to trudge the sparse, exposed incline. Each semblance of a series of trail switchbacks we saw ended up a bum steer—a mere cow trail leading no further than the next patch of grass. So we did what any decent upstanding citizen would do when faced with chaos—we bushwhacked.

Or rather, the bushes whacked us. And we didn't remain "upstanding" too long either. We downshifted into a three-point crawl.

The upper bajada slope was armed to the teeth. Thorns, spines,

Waw Kiwulik (Baboquivari Peak) viewed from the Sonoran Desert floor.

and stickers of every kind came with the sprawling ocotillo, wait-a-minute bushes, Palmer's century plants, desert spoons, cholla, prickly pear, barrel, rainbow, and saguaro cactus. I looked uphill and into the future—nights at home pulling the desert's vestiges out of my skin with tweezers. A white-necked raven flew over us, laughing.

As the going got tougher, we were presented with a greater view and stopped often to savor it. We could scan all the small dendritic drainages weaving down from the western slopes and draining into *Wamulĩ* Wash, an intermittent stream that fed Papago fields for centuries. And to the east we could see just the top of the granite obelisk known as Baboquivari Peak.

Or *Waw Kiwulik*, as the Papago say today, "rock drawn in at the middle." A name destined to be mangled by every foreign tongue that ever tried to shape its sound. To confuse matters more, the Papago word for rock cliff has changed its sound from "Vav" to "Waw" over the last two centuries. Around 1700, the explorer Padre Kino first wrote the name down as *Baggiburi*, using it to describe a village of 500 between the range and *Wamulĩ* Wash. By 1771, the *Sierra del Babuguiburi* was registered on maps, afloat in the *tierra incognita* of Papago Country. Even today, *Baboguivari* sits awkwardly on some U.S. maps, just as remote from the original Papago words as the official United States Geological Survey place name of Baboquivari.

The Papago description of the rock "drawn in at the middle" refers to a time when the peak was twice its size, shaped like an hourglass. The Papago farming along *Wamulĩ* Wash were many, and they felt they needed more farmland in the valley. So four elders went to visit *I'itoi* in the cave to ask him to move the mountains back so that the valley would be bigger.

I'itoi said that they must make cactus wine in four days. Then they must drink it, dance, and sing over the next four. Each day they drank and carried on more wildly, and the mountains began to soften and teeter. On the fourth day near dusk, the peak rocked until the top fell over, and the whole range moved, making *Wamulĭ* Valley wider.

Cloud Man, who lived up in the mountains, did not like this earth-shaking change, brought about by the greed of the people. He had to carry water from the mountains and did not appreciate that he would now have to travel further. In addition, he refused to bring more water to supply the additional land. The Desert People were never able to bring their newly gained land into cultivation, for without more water the land was useless. And the mountain that had looked like an hourglass had lost the shape for which it was named.

We finally turned our backs on the panorama, to climb the last stretch to the cliffs. Coyote's tobacco, coral bean, four wing saltbush, and hopbush grew in pockets above the thornier scrub. We reached the base of the thousand-foot cliffs and looked down again. We were now a thousand feet above the desert floor.

Searching for over half an hour, we came upon nothing that looked like a shrine. There were small overhangs and caves, but none of them were *I'itoi*'s. The sun was nearly down. Scratched, tired, and frustrated, we decided that we should head back down the forty-five degree slope and try another time.

Then Baptisto stopped us.

"Do you hear that?"

We listened. It was Salvador's voice, hundreds of feet below, singing to *I'itoi*. Down in the canyon, we could see a campfire he had made.

"Did you look on the other side of those white streaks on the cliff?" Baptisto asked.

We scrambled back along the base of the cliffs, eastward, toward the peak. We checked out three or four possible spots with no luck. Baptisto listened again. "He's singing us a path."

Suddenly, behind a jojoba bush, the last rays of the day's sun flashed on an opening in the rock. Then the sun was gone. A vertical slit beginning waist high allowed passage through a vein of brecciated porphyry. The entrance was only a foot and a half wide; we had to slide through on our sides.

Our eyes adjusted to the darkness. There, hanging above our heads from the cave ceiling, were rosary beads, chains with rings on them, and shoelaces. At our feet were a jar of saguaro cactus syrup and a green frog figurine—an effigy also found in prehistoric desert shrines. The walls of the cave had medallions, bullets, chewing gum, and cigarettes stuck in little niches. We placed some coins there, and then I decided to leave my cap, remembering a story of an entire Civil War uniform, cap and all, found there in the 1930s.

The cave was at least twenty feet deep, but we couldn't really tell how big it was—it didn't matter. We were on the edge of a place, a being that was larger and deeper than we were.

And that was it—recognizing that even though we had found the cave, it was still largely unknown to us. We were standing in the cool musky air of a sanctuary that was saying to us:

"There is always something hidden in this world, that you can't just realize from the outside. You need to make contact with it now and then, to nod your head in knowing, to receive its blessing."

We stood in the darkness, panting and shivering. Taken in by the mountains. Taking in the breath of I'itoi.

CHAPTER 2

Throwing Up the Clouds

Cactus Wine, Vomit, and Rain

Whoever established this liquor drinking for us, did so that we might ask for rain. That is its purpose. For we have no rivers and therefore must obtain rain.

PAPAGO MAN, SANTA ROSA

To the outside world, the Papago are best known as the Southwest Indians who harvest the fruit off columnar cactus. For decades, the gaudy color pages of *Arizona Highways* and *Desert* magazines have recorded this quaint practice. Imagine lovely young Indian maidens reaching poles up to pick saguaro fruit just as a tutti-frutti sunset breaks on the horizon.

It is a bit unsettling, then, when one comes upon today's desert fruit gatherers: cranky, weather-beaten old ladies, and reluctant teenagers worried about their skin getting too black from the sun. Most of what might have been picturesque has already melted in the Sonoran Desert's 115-degree summer heat. What persists are sweating Indians wearing sunglasses, plodding through the dry brush to camps cluttered with cans, bottles, and makeshift furniture. Their attitude toward cactus fruit is not exactly that of your typical natural food fanatic, seeking out some fresh, wholesome treat. They will be fermenting the fruit pulp for ceremonies in which nearly as much wine is thrown up as is swallowed down.

Call it the unsung side of the cactus ritual; it is the only side I know. The images that the color photos gloss over are the ones that have been burnt into my mind on these hellaciously hot summer days. The persistent perspiring and panting in the midst of the saguaro forests—they are part of the raw intimacy the Papago maintain with the desert. Somewhat ugly to the outside eye, this routine is an honest indicator of the strong bonds between the Desert People and their surroundings. Instead of running away from the desert during its driest, hottest time, some still run to the heart of it.

The special relationship of the Papago with the saguaro cactus characterizes their response to an arid homeland. Saguaros are not seen as a "separate" lifeform at all, not something of an "other," outside world. Papago classify saguaros as part of humankind; a saguaro cactus is "that which is human and habitually stands on earth." It is not, I believe, that saguaros are likened to humans because they often have "arms" coming off their upright trunks. It strikes me that the Papago liken saguaros, *Carnegiea giganteus*, to *Homo sapiens* because no matter how much they tend to dominate a landscape, they are still vulnerable.

Saguaros are referred to as humans because of their role in a parable which actually illustrates human fallibility. As Ruth Underhill transcribed the legend:

> A baby was deserted by his mother who was so enthusiastic about playing the game of double ball that she never nursed her child. The infant, after following her in vain, finally sank into the earth and came up on a mountain slope as a giant cactus. The people searched for it and finally the Crow [Raven] found it. The Crow flew to its summit (the giant cactus is often twenty to thirty feet high); it nibbled the fruit and vomited the red pulp into a basket. The people then put this pulp into a jar and said to it: "You know what to do." The pulp began to ferment, singing:
> "Here I stand,
> The wind is coming toward me,
> Shaking.

Here I stand,
A cloud is coming toward me,
Shaking."

The story goes on to tell how the drunkenness which the cactus wine brings is finally accepted. It is thereafter communally used to incite summer rains that the Desert People need in order to plant their crops. Yet the gifts of vomited fruit, of wine, and of rain ironically come as the result of human negligence—the desertion of a precious life which the earth fortunately takes in and transforms.

I was startled when I came upon some Papago who clearly take heed of the "human" vulnerability of saguaros. I heard a young city boy ask an elderly Papago woman if, lacking a harvesting pole, one could ever collect fruit off the tall cacti by throwing rocks at the tops to knock the fruit down.

"NO!" Marquita replied with a strain of horror in her voice. "The saguaros—they are Indians too. You don't EVER throw ANYTHING at them. If you hit them in the head with rocks you could kill them. You don't ever stick anything sharp into their skin either, or they will just dry up and die. You don't do anything to hurt them. They are Indians."

Such an eloquent plea for the protection of nature comes from a septuagenarian who can dance or drink me under the table any day. Marquita Gila, as one of the most frequently consulted Papago "informants," typically charges a flat fee for interviews: a case of Coors tallboys, which she affectionately refers to as "holy water." Since a mutual friend of ours drank herself to death at age twenty-nine, I've told Marquita I don't have the heart to provide alcohol for any Indian binges. She accepts this, but also expects me to bring her plenty of basketry materials, storage containers, and old-time seeds as gifts to take the place of that liquid token of cooperation.

In late June, I visited Marquita's camp outside of Snowbird City. I went along with a group of eager learners from the Snowbird Cactophiliac Society. If any of the Cactophiliacs were expecting to find a plump, redskinned Euell Gibbons in the form of Marquita, the afternoon must have seemed like a sweltering trip into chaos for them. No Euell Gibbons, nor any noble savages appeared.

As we piled into Marquita's camp, she was harping at the grandchildren who were supposed to be helping her. "Queek! Get some more wood! The fire is dying. Mona, grab hold of that handle. It's time to pour." And as one big pot of water, saguaro fruit pulp, and seeds was poured through a screen to separate out the seeds, she noticed another one bubbling up and burning. "Queek, queek, you boys! Move it off!"

She handed me a Rose brand flour sack and a couple sticks of saguaro ribs and said, "Make that strainer like I showed you last time." I slid the sticks under the lip seam of the sack, making handles with which to billow the bag open. I handed it to the two Papago girls, who held it over a large pail.

"Hold it open real far. Leon, help me pour—It's steel hot—No! You're messing it up! It's dreeping out—Not my fault—Not me. Oh, ṣo'ig añĭ. Poor me—"

As the kids finally took over watching the fire, and cleaning utensils, Marquita dragged herself over to the bed under the ramada, and slumped into it.

"You bring me any ice water? My boys went to town last night and forgot to bring me any ice back. Oh, ṣo'ig añĭ. And it was my birthaday!"

I came toward her with a dipper of water. "And you, *Milga:n Wakial.*—" (Her son had nicknamed me Gringo Vaquero.) "—Don't come near me looking big-eyed like that. I'm too old to give birthaday keeses anymore—Heh, heh, heh."

The Papago youngsters roared into laughter with that thought.

The Desert Smells Like Rain

Tasting *bahidaj si:tol* (saguaro cactus syrup), using a saguaro-rib stirring rod.

The eager Cactophiliacs were taken aback a little; then one politely asked how old she was now.

"I'm sixty-two," Marquita mumbled. At the same time, Popover, the Cactophiliac guide, said something in the background about Marquita being seventy last year.

"You could never guess that you were anywhere that old just looking at you—" one Cactophiliac beamed. No, not unless you looked hard enough to see the white roots under the Clairol black shiny hair, or noticed the pearly set of false teeth. "You must stay young because you live so close to the earth."

"Yes, that's right," Marquita said, dismissing the topic. "Popover, forget any more ice water. I need some holy water instead." A grandson handed her a Coors tallboy. Looking at all the perplexed faces around her, she just sat back and laughed. "Heh, heh, heh-heh."

There under the ramada of mesquite posts and plywood, twelve people and one puppy crammed themselves into the shade. A card table, three foldups, the bulging single bed, and an ice chest served as furniture. A fruit crate was hung from one of the upright posts, serving as a shrine with a metal crucifix, a porcelain Virgin Mary, and a bottle of Excedrin displayed inside. On a second post, a cross made of cottonwood leaves was hung to keep the lightning away from the camp. A third post had a battery-powered clock; guests were always looking for its electrical cord. "We just plug it into a saguaro cactus to recharge it," Marquita said with a Coyote look in her eyes; "that's what they call Indian Power."

Marquita has been coming to collect saguaro fruit here since long before the developers complicated things by building trailer courts and apartments at Snowbird City. Her grandfather used to bring her here by horse-drawn wagon, as part of their month-long loop through the gathering grounds around the Snowbird Valley. She personally has collected cactus fruit near this site for over sixty years. It is one of the most productive stands of saguaros anywhere. As Popover tells the Cactophiliacs, there are so many saguaros around Marquita's camp that it's "Standing Room Only."

The saguaro fruit picking and syrup making goes on, in spite of (or sometimes because of) all the attention. Energetic anthropologists come out and measure the distances Marquita walks between the cactus whose fruit she picks—she averages forty feet at the season's peak, but typically goes over a hundred feet in late July as the ripening peters out. Journalists ask her how much fruit it takes to make a quart of *si:tol* syrup—two buckets of raw fruit, to which another bucket of water is added, and then boiled down. When they ask her how long it takes, she says "That depends on how many reporters are around."

Tourists return year after year, asking to buy a pint of syrup to take back to Michigan or Kansas. "Well, we sold them for seven dollars a pint yesterday, but now everybody says ten dollars. A lotta work, you know." Back in 1929, the syrup was sold for the outrageous price of fifty cents a quart. Sometimes Marquita forgets how much work she did put into each little jar, and gives her enthusiastic visitors some to take home free. "I can always make more tomorrow."

But the last of the syrup made is never sold nor given away; it is kept in jars to be taken back to the Reservation. There, one or two mornings near the end of the season, a wagon still comes around in a few of the villages, to collect each family's donation of saguaro syrup.

These are taken away to the rainmaking camp, and put into a round brush house, or *olas ki:*. This is the stuff that sacred wine is made of.

We drove west early one hot August day, watching the few scattered clouds and mirages hovering on the horizon. Marquita had asked Popover to take her to harvest the fruit on the organpipe cactus, *cucuwis*, down near the border. I met Popover and Molly at their ranch in Snowbird, then we trucked out to the Reservation, where we picked up Marquita and her family.

Fifteen miles west past Sells, Marquita caught sight of a roadside flour sack that changed our day's plans. "TURN, Popover, that way!" Suddenly we were roaring down a dirt road to one of the few remaining saguaro wine feasts on the Reservation.

Other than the flour sack roadmarker, the Papago do not "advertise" the time or location of the wine serving, except as they have always done, by word of mouth. Once a Bureau of Indian Affairs superintendent arrested the instigators of these alleged "drunken orgies," but the courts ruled that the wine serving could not be stopped, due to its religious significance. Yet even among Papago, there is disagreement as to whether the wine-drinking for *I'itoi* contradicts or complements their Catholic faith. "They say it is like the ones that idolize the golden calf in the Bible," one old man told me. "I still believe in Jesus and the saints, but I know too that when we drink the wine and sing for *I'itoi*'s help, the rains always come."

Unlike the Pueblo Indian ceremonials, the Papago wine feasts have never been "spectator events" that whites were welcome to watch. Nevertheless, we were surprised when we arrived at the end of the dirt road: of the hundred or so pickups that had drawn up there in a broad semicircle, ours was the only one that carried whites as well as Indians.

This feeling of being a minority did not overwhelm us so much as the size of the ceremonial place itself. A circle hundreds of yards across had been cleared of every obstruction, so that even the curving line of parked pickups looked dwarfed in the spaciousness of the opening. Within this huge, packed-dirt arena, a ceremonial round house, *olas ki:*, and a mesquite and brush ramada, *wa:tto*, had been built. The ashes of a fire from the night before marked the ground a few feet from the *wa:tto*.

At dawn, following the second night of crossways dancing, the medicine man made his prophecy. A sprinkle would come that day, and a downpour in four more days. That downpour would make the washes run with enough water to allow people to plant their fields with a chance of success.

Now the people were assembling to sit and drink on the ground in a large circle just to the east of the *wa:tto*. Marquita's daughter signaled to us to come. Three or four medicine men were seated at each of the four cardinal directions. We moved in to sit on the east side of the circle, the direction from which we had come.

When the circle filled up, two elderly men came out of the *olas ki:* and greeted the gathering. They spoke slowly, with dignity, and related the origins and antiquity of the wine feast. It was not simply for getting drunk, they stressed, but for bringing the rains so that the plants could grow again.

One of the elders, leaning on a saguaro rib, acknowledged to the young people that the importance of the rains has diminished, since few families plant their floodwater fields anymore. Nevertheless, he felt it necessary to continue with this ritual for those who had planted in the past, and for the few traditional farmers who have persisted. These men wished the congregation at each cardinal direction a year of peace and good weather, and then moved from the circle.

Then out of the roundhouse came young men carrying containers of wine. Each was taken to the medicine men at each cardinal point for a blessing. Each medicine man moved his fingers around the wine vessel, saying a prayer over it. He drank up a cup, then scooped up a palmful of wine and tossed it into the sky.

The blessed wine was then passed around the circle. As a carrier placed it before us, we called out, "My friend!" as he dipped a canful for each of us.

I was handed a six-ounce Hormel frankfurter can of *nawait*. I downed most of it in two chugs, but left a little in my mouth to let the taste register. Marquita whispered, "No, you can't just sip it, you gotta down it all." A young Papago with waist-length hair and a goatee laughed, telling us, "You gotta really drink, for the rain, you know," and put his index finger up in the air. Not a cloud in sight.

The medicine men followed the first round with a series of "sit and drink" songs. Choppy little songs intoned as one man would wave his hand to keep the beat, and the others would chime in, hoarsely. The people shouted out "Friends!" after each of the four songs, then the wine came around again.

The mockingbird orations followed, calling up images of powerful storms quenching the earth and bringing the desert back to life. After more salutations, the keepers of the wine returned to the *olas ki:*. The circle broke up into groups of eight to twelve people at each of the cardinal points. There, the eldest medicine man was directing the serving of additional drinks to those clustered around him.

They handed me an eight-ounce can of wine which took several swallows to finish. A blood color, the wine tasted to me more like a slightly sweet, dry white wine than a red. I couldn't be sure of its strength, because the pace of drinking was so different. As soon as one of us finished a can, the ceremonial servers would fill it up again for us or for someone else. Every couple of minutes, each of us was washing down another cupful.

Molly chugged one down and ended up giggling. Some young Papago men loosened up and asked, "Where you from?"

"Tucson," I answered.

"The big one or the little one? Hah!"

"The too big one."

"I know what you mean because I tried to drive all-a-way down that Speedway street once, and I just kept driving and driving and I never did reach the other side."

Then another Papago with a Central Arizona College tee shirt asked, "Why you here? You trying to be Indians or something?"

"No. We got friends here. Good Papago friends. Your people have been good to us."

The Desert Smells Like Rain

"Well, then you drink up to help your Papago friends. *Nawaj!*" and they offered us those gentle, limp handshakes typical of Papago.

Now wine servings were brought over from other circles. Under the *wa:tto*, a large woman with a scarf covering her hair came with a wine-drenched basket bowl. The basket was woven wine-tight, mostly made of black devil's claw fiber, and filled to the brim. She greeted us and dished the elders up a serving. She gave me an Ortega chile can full—it tasted sweeter, fruitier. She refilled my can and handed it back. I slowed up drinking the second helping, but it didn't matter—the alcohol was already reaching me. Popover giggled and told the woman, "*Gracias, pero no gracias*," on a refill.

The wine smell was everywhere: on our breaths, splashed into our clothes, and in the air. People sporadically talked with us, but mostly we just watched the afternoon roll slowly along, listening to the incantations rise from the old men lying down in the dust.

For the elders had begun gathering on the ground, arms around each other, singing sweet, ancient songs, weeping from the wine's effects as they sang. Songs addressing and arising out of drunkenness. One was drinking cactus wine, the next drinking Coors, the third with his mouth up to the sky, swallowing air so that he could finish another verse. Old *compañeros*, their hats tilted back, were intent on remembering the songs floating through their memories, releasing them again in the wine-saturated air.

Then I started to notice that the men would stagger off from the center of the circle, some to pee, but most of them to throw up. They would walk twenty steps or so out from the group, open their mouths to the ground, and out would splash a wave of cream-colored foam. They would turn around and come back into a circle to sing, froth still left on their lips.

I watched the elders and some of the middle-aged Papago do

this off and on between their bouts of drinking. It wasn't a hard coughing regurgitation—the liquid appeared to come up as easily as it went down. They vomited in the open, without any hesitancy, and were taken back into the embrace of the other singers just as openly. The smell was not repulsive, nor was it that much different from the fresh wine's aroma.

Dr. Andrew Weil reminds us that few cultures understand that regurgitation can relate to well-being.

> Vomiting is an ultimately anti-social act, at least in societies desirous of relegating natural functions to the obscurity of the lavatory, away from public view. Most of us have vomited only in association with illness and do not think of it as something we could feel good about, let alone practice openly.

But it became evident that many of Weil's hunches about other societies viewing vomiting as a ritual of renewal hold true among the Papago. Underhill commented that:

> . . . the liquor had no very high alcoholic content. So much of it must be drunk before there is any intoxication that its most usual effect is to make the drinker vomit. This is recognized as a ceremonial feature, and people say with pleasure, pointing out a man so affected: 'Look, he is throwing up the clouds.' The regular procedure during the twenty-four hours of feast is to drink, vomit, sleep, and drink again, until the result is a thorough purging.

The power of the wine as a purgative is likely due to its unstable quality. Fermented in just two to four days, it quickly changes from diluted syrup to wine and then to vinegar. Its magic is as perishable as manna. Some batches already have a vinegar aftertaste when they are drunk; several pints of alcohol and acetic acid elicit an immediate response.

As Andrew Weil has observed, "vomiting often brings instant relief and a sense of well-being to someone who has ingested substances that the body does not want to accept."

This purging and subsequent physical relief tie in so well with the ceremonial start of the Papago's annual cycle. As they are being cleansed, they are bringing in the rains to renew the land and to break the heat.

The physical act of vomiting is usually associated with two involuntary responses: an upswing in breathing, and involuntary tears, both of which tend to invigorate and cleanse the body, internally and externally. Weil adds that there are mental effects too: a stimulation of the medulla, with a feeling of "letting go," allowing a person "to experience reality in another way."

This other sense of reality puzzled Francisco Garcés, a Franciscan who came upon a wine serving held by the Papago's closest relatives, the Gila River Pima, in 1776:

> This extravagant shouting (*exorbitante griteria*), a thing foreign to the seriousness of the Pimas, I knew came from drinking, which produced various effects. Some came and took me by the hand, greeting me. One said, "I am Pedro's father." Another said to me, "Thou hast to baptize a child." Another, "This is thy home, betake not thyself to see the king, nor to Tucson." Others made the sign of the cross, partly in Spanish; so that though I felt very angry at such general drunkenness, there did not fail me some pleasure to hear the good expressions into which they burst, even when deprived of reason, and even more to see that no woman got drunk. Moreover, some women picked up the clothing and beads that their husbands threw off so they would not be lost. They led with their right hands the horses on which their husbands were mounted. The next day I complained of these excesses to the governor, who told me that it only happened a few times and in the season of the saguaro, and adding that it made his people vomit yellow and kept them in good health.

Looking down at the muddy puddles of vomit and spilled saguaro wine in the dirt, I noticed rain drops scattering, hitting the powdery dust. Looking up, I saw the shadow of a lone cloud dimming the feast camp for a few minutes, scattering a drizzle over us. One old Indian cowboy pulled his hat brim down, and prodded his boot heel into the soil as he spoke. "Every time I been here to sit and drink that wine, there comes a little rain. Sure feels good to get wet again."

The singers sang on with fervor, tears streaming from their eyes. Behind them, a lean old man threw up one more time, then rolled over into sleep. Head tossed back and mouth open to the sky, his snoring joined in with the singing. The raincloud flowed on across the dusky skies of *Papaguería*, refreshing the earth.

CHAPTER 3

What Do You Do When the Rain Is Dying?

The reason Elder Brother planned this was that some day in the future the earth was going to be burned up and the water in the sea dried up. And he also told that the rains would not come down all over the earth very often, only once in a while, and the crops that the people raised wouldn't be irrigated anymore by rain water.

We sat down beneath the feathery canopy of the lone mesquite tree in the middle of the Madrugada family's field, seventy-year-old Julian and me. The field was fallow; the *charco* reservoir next to it was dry. It was July. Julian shook his head, pulled his cowboy hat down over his eyes, tired of looking at the cloudless sky.

"Rain—that's the main thing in the desert." Although nearly deaf, he always spoke quietly, figuring that if he could hear himself, others could probably hear him too. "You just can't plant anything—without the rain coming—without those washes running—"

Julian had waited since San Juan's day in late June for the summer thunderstorms to come. He had sickled the weedy cover off his field, so that it was ready to plow and sow with the first deeply drenching rains and sheetflooding. His seeds lay ready, in the wheelbarrow at the edge of his storage room, each in a separate cache, each the culmination of hundreds of years of rigorous selection by the desert climate and discriminating *O'odham* farmers: brown and white tepary beans, sixty-day white flour corn, striped cushaw squash, white-seeded devil's claw, and Spanish-introduced melons. They lay in waiting. Over a month now without a sprinkle to settle the dust.

"Now—the rain—is DYING—Sometimes I feel so sad—I just stay here waiting—I don't do anything until those rains come—"

Yet the rains hadn't completely died. In early August, three storms brought more than an inch and a half of rain within a week. By the time I could travel the muddy road back to the Madrugada home, Julian had plowed and planted. That cluster of rains was enough to initiate sheetflow across thirty acres of desert floor, bringing water and nitrogen-rich debris into the half-acre field. The "run-on" soaked in to a depth of at least six inches. Judging by the feel of the soil, Julian had decided it was cool and moist enough to allow seeds to germinate. Runoff from the storm had also trickled down several shallow channels, and had been diverted into the *charco* by Julian's well-placed shovel work. The runoff had filled the hand-dug reservoir with enough water so that he could flood-irrigate the field a week later. He borrowed a neighbor's mule, which, teamed with his horse, pulled a walking plow to churn under the debris and seed to a depth of three to eight inches.

The Madrugada crops came up, as did the volunteers that are more frequent in Papago fields than they are in the surrounding desert. They included devil's claw, purslane, coyote tobacco, coyote melon, ground cherry, finger gourds, six-weeks grama grass, and the leafy amaranth known regionally as *quelite de las aguas*. The amaranths and several other of these volunteers come up thickly enough to be used as edible greens, the *i:waki* that once sustained the Papago between the cactus fruit harvest and crop maturation. Plant diversity in Papago fields appears to be greater than that in nearby Anglo fields and as high as on the wild desert flats. Julian worked to keep these volunteers from choking his crop plants, but also took bag-loads of the greens back to the house for his wife to prepare.

As the field plants grew, so did the number of animals attracted to them: black-tailed and antelope jack rabbits, desert cottontails, gophers, Gambel's quail, blackbirds, and white-necked ravens. I visited the Madrugada home in late September, after the season's rains had already ended. Margarita told me I could find her husband out in the field, and I thought I could see him as I looked out from the house. As I approached, I realized the figure standing in the field in Julian's faded jeans and flannel shirt was a makeshift scarecrow of saguaro cactus ribs, what the Papago call *Milon C-ed O'odham*, "In the Melon Patch People." Julian, slingshot dangling from his hand, was asleep on a mattress he had hauled out and put under the mesquite.

He stirred a little as I came near.

"Mr. Madrugada, I think I just heard one of those *Milon C-ed O'odham* snoring!"

"Ho! What's that?"

"You must be a pretty good shot to hit those animals with your eyes closed," I said, pointing to his slingshot. He laughed, then put on his best face of vigilance.

"No, but look what those rabbits did! They got to eating the tepary bean vines and gave those plants a real good haircut. Those *tobĭ*, they sure are mean!"

The Madrugadas felt they needed to fence the field with chicken wire to discourage rabbits. The food production and nutrition project I work with soon supplied them with some. Julian and his son quickly put it up, burying the bottom of the chicken wire in the ground so animals would have difficulty crawling under it. Just as they were finishing the last roll, they spotted a cottontail in the bean patch. Gathering up a few neighbors and a few sticks, they hunted it down as the *O'odham* had

One of the few crops domesticated north of Mexico, Devil's Claw is used
as a black basketry fiber.

harvested "field meat" for centuries. Circling around it and driving it toward one side, they rushed in and knocked it cold. The field yielded rabbit stew that night.

With the rabbit problem reduced, the teparies and corn made it to maturity by early October. However, the other crops were suffering. It hadn't rained for more than three weeks, and soil moisture was depleted. The pinto beans, an introduced variety, had withered and died. The squash, melons, and many of the weeds were badly wilted. As a last resort, Julian had begun hauling buckets of water over to the field, one by one over a path of more than fifty yards.

The plants revived. By mid-October, Julian was piling weeds up over the burgeoning fruit to hide it from the ravens. He had pulled up the tepary vines a week before, and plopped them upside down to dry in the sun. Now he was threshing them— beating the papery pods with a stick. The dried beans popped out and covered the tarp with a fine rain of color. The fruits of one old man's labor.

In December, I stopped by the Madrugadas after a brief winter rain. Would he be plowing again, planting the old Sonoran wheat, peas, and garbanzos? A drought had set in since September. Julian was out deepening his *charco*, shoveling the clay from the reservoir bottom up onto the dike that surrounded it on three sides. He leaned on the handle of the spade.

"My friend—I've been wondering where you were—because I've been wanting to talk with you—to tell you what I've been doing with the rain."

He took a deep breath, then continued. "See, I've been waiting for more rain to come—it's been so long, the ground is hot below—When it is hot underground and just a little rain comes, the heat comes up from below—It just dries the dirt out again.

"That's why we need more rain to come—to cool the earth so

that it will stay wet enough to let the seeds come up—to let them grow."

Enough rain didn't come to cool the earth until mid-February. When it had soaked in, Julian planted peas, corn, and beans: a mixture of winter and spring crops. He watched the sky for clouds that might build up into storms. . . .

While the Papago perceive the rain is dying, Anglo dwellers in the Sonoran Desert are now realizing that another water resource has been driven into a death march: groundwater reserves accumulated during the Ice Age are rapidly being depleted. As Chuck Bowden says in *Killing the Hidden Waters*, it has taken less than a century of groundwater pumping for modern Southwestern agriculture to deplete fossil water reserves that cannot now be recharged, and this has been done at the expense of precious fossil fuel as well. Seventy miles north of the reservation, water levels are dropping as much as twenty feet per year, due to a pumping rate nearly one hundred times that of natural recharge. In many places throughout southern Arizona, the cost of pumping is greater than the value of certain water-consumptive crops. Mexican arid lands expert Enrique Campos-Lopez predicted that by 1985, rainfall-based agriculture will again be more energetically attractive than mechanized, groundwater-irrigated agriculture on both sides of the border. Desert runoff farming is suddenly the "new idea" for hydrologists and crop scientists who live within an hour of Papago floodwater fields, but have never ventured out of their offices to see them.

Concomitant with the resurgence of interest in rainfall and floodwater harvesting is a new appreciation of the value of desert-adapted crops. Yet many of the traditional drought-hardy crop varieties fell out of use and became extinct when commercial agriculture based on pumping and hybrid crops was initiated earlier in this century. Papago, leaving their floodwater fields to work for wages in irrigated fields, lost many of their bean and corn varieties as the life of their remaining seeds expired while they were away. At the same time, their water control structures deteriorated, and the washes which fed them were disrupted by new roads and livestock ponds.

As Daniel Janzen points out, "What escapes the eye . . . is a much more insidious kind of extinction: the extinction of ecological interactions." Not just crops were lost—whole field ecosystems atrophied. Roughly 10,000 acres of crops were grown via Papago runoff farming in 1913; by 1960, there were only 1,000 acres of floodwater fields on the Papago Indian Reservation. Today, Papago sporadically farm less than 100 acres using floodwaters.

While the remaining acreage is minuscule, it is all that is left of an ecologically sensitive subsistence strategy that has endured in deserts for centuries. Here, not only a rich heritage of crops remains, but also co-evolved microorganisms and weeds, as well as pests and beneficial insects. Amaranths, for instance, are hosts for insects that control corn-loving pests. Papago fields harbor nitrogen-fixing bacteria which naturally associate with tepary bean roots. A species of solitary bee has been found visiting annual devil's claw in Papago fields, but despite a thorough search has not been found on wild annual devil's claw elsewhere. Moreover, there is a mutually beneficial relationship between these plants and their Papago stewards; the Papago have evolved field management skills that have allowed them to sustain food production for centuries without destroying the desert soils. The plants have evolved the ability to grow quickly, root deeply, disperse heat loads, and provide nutritious seeds for those who harvest them. These durable functional relationships between humans and other lifeforms are the products of a slow evolution and cannot be remade in a day. No amount of academic research on water harvesting and drought-hardy crops can replace a time-tried plant/man symbiosis such as that in which the Papago have participated.

By late April, the rains had waned again, and I wondered if the Madrugada crops would ever reach maturity. I visited the field with another scientist who was also interested in helping traditional desert-adapted agriculture to persist. We walked around and around the field and its rainfall catchment area, brainstorming on innovations that could make the system more effective or easier to manage for the old man. Julian and an elderly Papago friend stood and chewed the fat on the edge of the now-dry reservoir.

When we returned to where they stood, Julian set his cowboy hat back on his head and said, "Well, there—did you figure it out—how to make more water come to the field?"

"We're not sure," I replied sheepishly.

"Only one way—to do that—" he said, grinning. He looked at his friend and urged him on.

"You got to know the right old songs—"

"Then you just got to dance to bring down that rain!"

The old men lifted their feet, raised the dust on the *charco* bank, and laughed and laughed.

CHAPTER 4

Changos del Desierto

Growing Up on the Reservation

Sand was here. Then water came from the rain. Water was all over. When the water sunk in the sand, pretty plants came from the ground. A car came. One of the rabbits jumped out and went to a bush and had some babies.

MAKING A DESERT, CELESTINE PABLO, 1976

The babes of the desert sense early that they are in a place wildly alive. When I first worked on the Papago Indian Reservation teaching natural history writing at the boarding school, I was dumbfounded by the grade schoolers' impressions of the desert. I asked them to contrast the city with the desert; they called the desert noisy. The early morning chattering and chirping of Gila woodpeckers, cactus wrens, Gambel's quail, and thrashers made the city seem quietly lifeless in comparison. The desert was delicious and busy in their minds. One girl wrote, "I am a hummingbird and in the summer I like to hum all over the flowers and suck their sweet water." The desert is also fragrant and powerful; Carman Martin said of ṣegai, the creosote bush that covers the area surrounding the school: "Ṣegai smells like rain, and my mother told me it is medicine."

Though it seems forbiddingly arid to outsiders, Papago children feel the desert is suitable for many lifeforms. What's more, the world had to dry out before it could be lived in comfortably, as Timothy Garcia explains in this creation story:

Long time ago the desert was full of water, in fact, it was an ocean. The animals were on top of every mountain. They felt very sad, so they sent out the coyote to see if he could swim across to the other mountains. But when he did, the water disappeared and left the ground looking like a desert. All kinds of animals began to live in the ground. All the animals called this hot and rocky place the desert.

The Papago see the desert as more than just a stomping ground for common wildlife such as antelope jackrabbits, round-tailed ground squirrels, and turkey vultures. It is also the home of mythical animals. There is the owl that glows in the dark, a bad omen. The kids are fascinated by occasional sightings of a beast called "Hairy Man" that shows up in headlights at night and can outrun the fastest police car. The *Ñe:big*, a giant reptile, occasionally causes the ground to cave in. There are places where voices come up from the earth.

Some Papago children intentionally set out from human habitations to experience this wild world. One such precocious explorer was only two years old when he wandered away while visiting his grandmother's home out in the desert. Parents came out to check on him, thinking he was playing in the backyard, and suddenly realized he was out of sight. Frightened, five adults fanned out to search through the mesquite thickets of the braided washes behind the house.

After twenty minutes of looking, the grandfather thought he heard a small animal rustle in a nearby bush. But it wasn't a small animal—it was a small animal *hunter*.

The boy poked a saguaro rib—his pretend gun—out of his cover. He pulled a branch down, and two little eyes peeked out. Then he broke through the brush, slinging his gun over his shoulders, balancing it like a yoke.

"Hi, grandpa. I just been out hunting! Seen any animals out here?"

The Desert Smells Like Rain

While most Papago youngsters go out into the desert for play, some occasionally end up "lost" among the cactus and caliche. There was one such occurrence several years ago in the remote *ranchería* of Badger.

September 15th came on Badger like a hot iron. The temperature reached above 95 that afternoon. Though it hadn't rained since a downpour on the 12th, there was still a sauna-like mugginess in the rank roadside undergrowth. The earlier rains had released a flush of insects, which droned and moaned incessantly. For a hot, humid summer day in the Sonoran desert, nothing seemed amiss.

But the Badger community was in a state of disorder. Its youngest member, two-and-a-half-year-old Immanuel Pedro, was missing.

Manny had been playing with the dogs around noon when he was last seen. After his grandparents looked for him by themselves for more than an hour, they decided to call for help. By three in the afternoon, villagers from Badger and nearby San Luis formed to search the bajadas skirting the Comobabi Mountains. The Papago police were alerted, and they sought other assistance.

By dusk, there were dozens of Papago swarming the ocotillo hills of the mountain range. The Border Patrol, U.S. Customs, the Arizona Department of Public Safety, the Bureau of Indian Affairs Law Enforcement Office, and Papago Emergency Services all joined in the search.

By nightfall, they found Manny's sneakers a mile from home. They chanced upon his tracks as far as three miles from the village. Two of the three dogs that had left with him returned home tired and thirsty.

As darkness set in, no one had seen hide nor hair of Manny himself. The police passed out flashlights, and a dozen men kept searching.

At dawn, most of the party gathered back at the grandparents' place. Each man had hunches about where the lost boy might be.

One guessed that the remaining dog had led Manny to a nearby waterhole. But others had checked there and had seen no footprints. Still others hoped that the boy had stumbled onto the road to San Luis and would be found there. As they were having coffee and pinole for breakfast, the bad news came from San Luis: Manny was not there.

Manny's grandmother broke down. As she later confessed to a journalist:

"I was going out of my mind. I thought they would find him during the day. At night I thought they would never find him again."

The searchers began the second day with dread, a few grimly seeking out spots where vultures were circling.

Somewhere in a sandy wash, Manny was waking up, feeling the belly of the panting dog next to his face. In socks scratchy with stickers, shorts and tee shirt stuck to his sweaty back, he sat up and wiped the sand from his eyes. After a while, he started walking again, followed by his dog.

Manny and the dog wandered along off and on throughout the second day. Now he felt tired all the time, his throat itched, and the droning bugs were giving him a headache. They rested several times in the shade of mesquite trees, until the flies came and made Manny too miserable to stay.

Soon he began to hear another kind of buzzing. The Arizona Department of Public Safety had called in its emergency helicopter. The Border Patrol had brought up its airplane.

As the second night approached, Manny stretched out to nap again. As the shadows were moving in, a Border Patrol plane spotted a dog walking circles around a body lying on a mound of earth. They radioed the nearest ground search team to see if the boy was still alive.

When the Border Patrol approached the mound, the dog ran to face them, teeth flashing. Barking and growling, the dog kept them at bay. Manny barely moved. The search party frowned, and one man mumbled something about shooting the dog.

Then the helicopter whipped over the ridge and hovered down into the clearing to land. The startled dog retreated to Manny's side. A paramedic bounded out of the helicopter, picked Manny up, took him back, and handed him to the pilot. Before the medic could climb back in, the dog leapt into the helicopter ahead of him.

When Manny's grandparents heard over the police radio that the aircraft had found him, they crossed themselves and prayed. They went outside to await the helicopter. But as they watched the copter rise out of some hills five miles away, they saw it go off in another direction. Grief-stricken, the grandmother broke down again and had to be helped inside.

Two hours later, after a brief checkup at Tucson Medical Center where he was found "slightly worn, but in good health," the boy and his dog were returned home. The Badger community was made whole again.

"He was way off in the other direction from where he could have gotten water," Papago officer Ed Noriego told me later. "How he stayed alive is a mystery, even with the dog protecting him."

Surviving in the desert heat for even a day without water is no easy trick. The stresses are tough for an adult, let alone for a two-and-a-half-year-old child. Yet once you know the degree of dehydration that adults can tolerate, Manny's September meander becomes all the more remarkable.

Desert ecologist Schmidt-Nielson gives as a rule of thumb that "a man is physically and mentally unable to take care of himself at ten percent weight loss, and at about twelve percent water deficit he is unable to swallow and can no longer recover without assistance."

For a 200-pound man, this provides considerable leeway, since a twenty-pound water loss is substantial. In fact, a "normal European" adult can survive two days in desert temperatures of 100–110°F with no water at all but then needs a minimum of a gallon a day. Although in rare cases men have endangered themselves by sweating off as much as twenty-four pounds of water in a day, typically no more than ten pounds are lost even by men actively traveling in the desert.

But what are the limits for a child who weighs only twenty-five pounds? According to the rule of thumb, if he lost as much as two to three pounds of water—around a quart and a half—he would be imperiled. Through urinating a few times over his thirty-hour span in the desert, and by being exposed to the sun for a mere five or six hours, Manny could have easily given back at least that much water to the earth and sky. Was his little body breaking or escaping the rules? Or did the dog find water for Manny along the way? How did he survive when death from water loss was all but inevitable?

Ask the dog about it. Or shout the question out across the desert flats, and listen until the earth issues up an answer. . . .

Sooner or later, Manny and other children like him choose where they will live. The desert remains a friend or becomes a foe. Many Papago youngsters choose to leave their grandparents' world behind early in their lives. By the time some of them reach age ten, they are long gone.

Yet a few hang on to something their grandparents have told them, or to a familiar feel in the desert air. They hang onto it as it bucks and sunfishes and takes them on journeys of a kind the others will certainly miss.

On a brisk October morning at the boarding school, a secret meeting of brothers is being called. Third grader Felix Lambert walks over to where first grader Jeffrey is eating Cheerios and whispers, "Go into that bathroom over there."

Jeffrey leaves his cereal bowl to meet his brother by the toilets. "We gotta get out of here. They're coming to take our pee-churs."

"Huh?" Jeffrey is still a little sleepy.

"Those white men are coming to take our pee-churs today in the classes. Remember what Grandma say?"

"Uh uh. Huh?"

"She say not to let them take your pee-churs or you never grow old like her. That's how come she's a little old lady like that."

"How come?"

"They never took her pee-churs!"

"*He'e:*! Where do we go?"

Within five minutes the brothers have sneaked off the school grounds, running north up a wash, ducking overhanging branches of mesquite. By eight they are nearly a mile north of the school, where the wash crosses the road leading up to Casa Grande. They hide in a culvert at the side of the road.

"Where we going?" Jeffrey asks again, panting.

"Up to the village," Felix finally whispers, revealing what little plan he has.

"What if a car comes, and it got a *Milga:n* inside it and he takes us over to school, and instead of getting home, they take our pee-churs?"

Felix frowns. "Just gotta watch the way they drive."

The first car going north roars as it approaches them. They hide, scared, until just as it whizzes past, Felix glances up at the passenger.

"See? That was a *Milga:n*. Drive real fast."

Soon another big car comes speeding by them. A little braver this time, Felix catches a good look at the driver of the Pontiac.

"Hmmm. That was an Indian, though he sure drives like a white man. Must be late for work, or something."

The next vehicle can be heard from miles away as it approaches. With a bad muffler and a cold engine, it sounds like a hesitant round of firecrackers exploding.

The Desert Smells Like Rain

"Come on!" Felix yells, and they jump up on the road. It seems that the truck is taking forever to reach them.

The old Ford pickup has an elderly Papago man coaxing it along. He almost fails to see them, then swerves, brakes, and rolls to a halt about forty feet past the culvert. They run and climb into the pickup bed.

"You *changos*. Too cold out there. Come up here."

They crawl up into the cab, slam the door, and sit politely next to the old man. He shifts, and the truck lurches into movement again.

About three miles up the road, the old man asks the inevitable: "Where you going?"

"We quit that school. They were gonna take our pee-churs!" Jeffrey blurts out as Felix frowns, furious. The older boy nonchalantly adds, "Oh, we're just going up there to the village on that side," pointing west of the road miles to the north.

"Pee-churs, huh?" the old man muses, driving along. "I always been too ugly for them white men to want to take my pee-churs. Never had no problem. No one ever did take one of those of me. I still got my soul because of that."

The boys look at him, silent. A white-haired, wrinkled-up old man. He sure *is* ugly, just as he said, but he's old too. That must mean something.

The boys have the old man let them off nearly a mile beyond the road running west to the Burnt Place, their village. This way they avoid traffic—including any people from the school looking for them. The spot where they are left is just desert. Felix looks out across the valley to the mountain range on the other side. He scans the horizon until he hits upon a familiar notch in the rock. He knows that the village should be four or five miles away, between that notch and where they stand. They set off toward the village.

As they bushwhack to escape the school, the desert opens up to them. They see a dead giant saguaro cactus, its exposed ribs arching out into the sky like a fountain. They find a huge mesquite tree, with hundreds of turkey vulture feathers under it. They pick from its branches handfuls of sweet red-speckled pods which they chew on as a snack food. They watch a shrike impale a lizard on the thorns of an ocotillo. Jeffrey scares them both by inadvertently stepping on a locoweed pod, which pops like a firecracker.

"I thought it was the school shooting at us," Felix laughs, as he and Jeffrey stuff their pockets full of other locoweed pods to stomp on later.

Meanwhile, back at the boarding school, the teachers were figuring out that both Lambert boys were missing. When the third grade teacher came to Felix Lambert during roll call, one of his friends replied, "He ain't comin'." The other students giggled.

It was not until coffee break that the teacher discovered that both boys were missing, and that no one had come for them. The teachers alerted the truant officer, who said that he was going up toward Casa Grande later in the day anyway, and he would check with the boys' family at the Burnt Place. They also contacted the Tribal Police and the Community Health van drivers to watch out for two boys on the road. The teachers returned to their classrooms and lined the children up to have their photographs taken.

Around three in the afternoon, two laughing, mud-covered boys come running up to the top of the flood control levee on the east side of the village. They look out over the whole place—the mesquite log corral, the chapel, the skeleton of the old stone school, and the baseball field with its three ramadas. The boys dart straight toward the back of their family's house, glad to be home. The door gets bigger with every step. As they come through the door, they see that a stranger is sitting at the table, and a big government car is waiting outside the front doorway.

"Come on, boys, change your clothes if you have any extras

here, and I'll drive you back to school. We should get back in time for you to play a little baseball before dinner."

The boys turn to their mother and grandmother. The two women are silent, looking down at the floor.

"Okay, mister. Mister, do you know something? Do you know if that man who takes the pee-churs still gonna be there?" Grandma perks up.

"No, I don't think so. I think it was his car that was ahead of me on the road north from the school. He must have been going back to Casa Grande."

"Okay, mister, we gotta take these muddy jeans off. Come on, Jeffrey, 'cause then we gotta go with that man."

The boys go into the next room and start to giggle. Jeffrey steps on a locoweed pod that fell from his pocket, and they giggle even harder. Now that they know they won't be photographed, they put on their favorite home clothes and return to the main room. Jeffrey looks at Grandma, who is smiling at him—she sure is *old*.

That even fairly young children know how to beat the system may come as a surprise. But the Papago don't call their mischievous young ragamuffins *changos* for nothing—it is in part to recognize that they are "monkeying around" with cleverness and humor. Although few Papago have ever seen real monkeys, they long ago borrowed this Spanish term and applied it to a native animal with the same prankish character—the coatimundi. Occasionally sighted in the Baboquivari range, coatis are notorious for making mayhem among garbage, food caches, and crops. It seems the Papago children are seen both like coatis and mythical monkeys when an adult today calls them *changos*.

At the same time, Papago love kids above all else in life. This feeling comes out in the story of the Children's Shrine, an altar where at one time the Papago made a grave sacrifice in order to save the world. On a floodplain near Santa Rosa, the shrine is

A monument in the center of *A'al Hihi'añ*, the Children's Shrine, indicates where four children were sacrificed to prevent the desert from being flooded.

a pile of rocks surrounded by a five-foot-tall semicircle of dead ocotillo shoots forming a wall against the wind.

One June day, I was driving by the shrine with Gregorio, Isidro's youngest boy. We decided to go over to the shrine, because Gregorio had never seen it. He stood by it awhile, glancing around at the ancient ocotillo wall that had piled up in ceremonies over many decades. Gregorio was curious about the gifts to the shrine left atop the cairn—a bracelet, a picture of a dark girl in a wedding dress, a half-dollar coin, ribbons, baby toys, and feathers.

"Why do they give these things?" he asked.

So I told him what I could remember of what they say happened there long ago. In a time of famine and drought, a hunter sinned by chasing a badger down into its hole. The hole broke open, and wind and water began pouring out. The headman desperately called in the *mamakai* to do their medicine and singing to stop these things from roaring out of the ground. On four consecutive days, four medicine men each tried to stop the gushing, but they were not strong enough. It looked as though the world would be destroyed in the storm and flood.

Finally, one who was not a medicine man spoke up: "We must give to this place in the earth our most valuable possession—our children. Then perhaps the water and wind will stop roaring out of the hole, destroying the land."

The people agreed that as their last chance, they would give up what meant the most to them. Four children—two girls and two boys—were dressed up, and began dancing around the hole. As they circled it, they slowly sank into the earth, and the gushing stopped. The world was saved.

They are still alive in the earth today. And when it rains, you can hear their voices coming up from the hole beneath the cairn.

Gregorio looked at me wide-eyed. "But what can we give?"

He paused for a moment, then pulled from his throat a neck

chain with a tooth hanging from it—a gift that his brothers gave him for his birthday just a month ago. Before we left, we placed all the change in our pockets, a ripe saguaro fruit, and a cowboy hat on the shrine, too. As we drove away, Gregorio's head was poked out the window, looking back at the shrine, reaching back into the mental pictures his ancestors had set up for their descendants long ago. Images in the desert to help them grow up strong, observant, and grateful.

CHAPTER 5

Raising Hell as Well as Wheat

Papago Indians Burying the Borderline

Entre las tribus indígenas más curiosas de nuestro país, sobre-
salen los Pápagos. Son 800 nada más y ocupan zonas desérticas
de Sonora. Los Pápagos no se consideran ni norteamericanos
ni mexicanos pero sí legítimos dueños de Sonora y Arizona.

EL IMPARCIAL, THE HERMOSILLO NEWSPAPER

Isidro Saraficio is sitting in a dry irrigation ditch, under the shade
of a Mexican elderberry tree, gazing out over a wheatfield wa-
vering in the noonday heat. It's a fine stand of wheat for a desert
field grown with just the rain that ran down the arroyos this winter. Isidro diverts floodwaters from a holding pond to the field
through hand-dug ditches, letting gravity rather than machines
do the work. Now that the grain is ripe, his friends have come to
the *ranchería* to help with the harvest. After working since dawn,
they lie resting, some snoring or farting in their sleep, while di-
gesting the lunch of beans, *carne asada*, chile, tortillas, and beer.
The cool shade of the elderberry soothes them for a few minutes
more before they return to the wheat patch, armed with sickles,
to hand-harvest the grain.

The quiet of noon is suddenly ruptured. Like a giant raptor, a
Border Patrol plane breaks into sight and roars down across the
land a few hundred feet over the field, causing quail and doves
to flush out of the wheat. The patrolling plane zips westward,
straight above the fence line and firebreak that stretches as a scar

all the way to the far horizon. Sitting up as if awakening from a bad dream, Isidro's friends realize that the nightmare sound they heard is part of his everyday world. The field lies within a half mile of the U.S./Mexico border.

Isidro planted the wheat not only for *pinole* and popovers, but also as a political protest. He was born here on the ranch in Sonora, Mexico, when the elderberry above him first came into bloom thirty-four years ago. Yet his family has never had a deed to this place, which they have probably farmed for hundreds of years. Isidro has planted wheat on land that another man "legally" owns. The field has been worked to show that the homestead has not been deserted. Isidro "borrowed" a tractor from a U.S. high school and illegally drove it across the border to plow the field while it was still sufficiently wet to plant. Now, six months later, his Arizona friends come through the fence as "reverse migrants" without visas or permits, neither reporting to customs nor paying any respects to the international line.

In short, Isidro is raising hell as well as wheat. He is raising his sickle to question the existence of a boundary that his people have never acknowledged.

Isidro is a Papago Indian, sharing this borderland dilemma with 10,000–15,000 of his people who refer to themselves as the *Tohono O'odham*. When seventeenth-century Catholic missionaries made their first *entradas* into the Sonoran Desert, they found Papago settlements in many of the places they remain today. As northern Mexico and the U.S. Southwest became Spanish colonies, the Papago adopted many Hispanic customs and technologies. To most outsiders, a place such as Isidro's looks less American Indian than Mexican.

In 1853, a political decision made thousands of miles away divided the Papago country between the United States and Mexico. Under the Gadsden Purchase, more than 5,000 square miles of Papago homeland became part of the United States. Although the majority of Papago were now nominally under the jurisdiction of Washington, they continued to associate more with the Indians and mixed-descent *mestizos* south of the border than with other U.S. citizens. As late as 1900, there were still enclaves of Papago miles north of the international border who thought of themselves as Mexican.

Yet, as more economic opportunities became available for Papago workers in the United States, population shifts occurred. Families that had remained in their desert *rancherías* on both sides of the border now migrated to U.S. towns and artificial agricultural oases which the Anglos had created with dams and wells. Today, three-quarters of the Papago people live on three reservations established for them, and fewer than a tenth of them remain in Mexico.

Isidro's family was one of the minority that chose to stay in Sonora. Isidro's father did send the boy across the border to a Catholic boarding school to learn to read and write, but the family remained at the ranch in Plenty Coyotes village, just south of the U.S. Papago Indian Reservation on the border. Then Isidro's mother died and he came home from school to live alone with his father for eight years, helping the old man with farming, ranching, and blacksmithing. When the elderly Saraficio died several years ago, Isidro and a brother inherited the family homestead.

Isidro quickly realized that although the inheritance was strong in his heart, it was weak in the courts of Mexico. The people of Plenty Coyotes are part of those called "two-village Papago," for they spend part of the year in their fields, and part at a well village miles away. When the official Mexican surveyors came through the borderland deserts years ago, they found what they presumed to be abandoned fields, and reported them as "open land." While the Papago families who had worked these lands for centuries were just a few miles away, the land was deeded to new

Ocotillo, mesquite, saguaro ribs, and dry earth are the key materials for the walls of a native Sonoran Desert dwelling.

owners, one a wealthy rancher who spends most of his time in U.S. cities. This landlord, Juan Stone, now uses 172,000 acres of land that traditionally belongs to the Papago.

Isidro began to inquire among the authorities about how an absentee landowner could retain so much land under the land reform laws. While he was still under thirty, the Sonoran Papago elected him as their representative in order to challenge the Mexican government's neglect of Papago interests. After more than a dozen journeys to Mexico City to plead the Papago case, Isidro bitterly realized that the bureaucracy does not budge easily. The Papago in Sonora could not be given government assistance in land and water resources improvement unless they legally owned the land. And when Isidro argued that they had prior claim to the land, some officials questioned whether any Papago lived in Mexico historically—hadn't they filtered down from "the other side"?

Infuriated, Isidro left his position as representative of the Papago in Mexico to study the historic sources which documented the early *O'odham* distribution in the Sonoran Desert. Working in the Catholic mission archives in Arizona, Isidro set out to prove his people's rights to the Sonoran lands that were part of their heritage. Yet most of the social and political scientists who usually assist Indians in these cases were either ignorant or noncommittal. One sheepishly admitted that "Juan Stone's wealthy friends in the Southwest do a lot to support our humanities programs here."

Isidro's effort finally began to be appreciated by the Papago politicians in Arizona. They were intrigued by his attempts to document the aboriginal territory of the Papago, but were not quite sure where his inquiries could lead. Finally, they began to listen to him, not as politicians listen to political radicals, but as tribal elders have always listened to those moved by a vision. Isidro was relatively young, but they felt that he spoke for hundreds of generations of *O'odham*.

Are not all Papago one people, wherever they live, bonded together by a common culture, language, history, and a sacred sense of community? Hasn't a simple line on a map disrupted this sense of community? Hasn't the international boundary kept Papago families from visiting sacred sites of Papago religion? Isn't the Papago tribe *less than whole* if it continues to let an arbitrary political decision divide its legacy, and dispossess part of its people? The Papago met in May 1979 and passed several resolutions which Isidro and others had drafted.

At the Sells Papago Capital Center, the Tribal Council declared that the Treaty of Guadalupe Hidalgo and the Gadsden Purchase which divided Papago country were signed without consultation or the consent of the Papago people. They agreed that to counter this historic tragedy, they would consider enrolling the Mexican Papago in the Arizona tribe so that they could share all benefits, including the $26 million land claims award granted to the tribe by the U.S. government.

The Council also requested of the Mexican government that the aboriginal lands in Mexico be set aside and reserved exclusively for the Papago, or that they be ceded or transferred to the U.S. in trust for the Papago. Isidro and his collaborators had hoped that this resolution would embarrass the Mexican government into confiscating the deeds from Stone and others in order to set up a reservation south of the border. Yet they kept open a more pragmatic possibility: if Mexico did not act soon, they would approach the absentee landlords and buy the deeds back with Arizona tribal funds, at whatever price. They would then turn over the deeds to Papago who had retained their Mexican citizenship. But the Mexican government responded at last. It helped obtain small land reserves around two Sonoran villages that the Papago could use exclusively.

Finally, the Tribal Council addressed the problem of the borderline touching the reservation, more than 60 miles of jurisdictional headache. They demanded of both national governments that Papago be given free access across the international boundary, so that their people would never be accused of being "illegal aliens" again. They also made clear that both governments had been negligent in maintaining the fence and protecting residents along the border.

Isidro was well aware of the smugglers that frequently crossed the border near his homestead. Drug runners and "coyotes" who piloted wetbacks across the border had realized that U.S. agents patrolled the Papago reservation less vigilantly than any other area along the boundary. The runners had not only cut through the boundary fence; they had cut dozens of field and range fences on Papago lands, allowing cattle to roam and destroy crops. The drug runners sometimes shot at anyone in sight—not just official-looking gringos, but unassuming Indians too. Isidro had been offered $10,000 a month or 5,000 head of cattle if he would let a crime ring use his homestead as a front.

"I could have been a rich man several times over," he told me once. "But is that a life for a family man? How could I do that to my kids?"

In a meeting with U.S. Customs and other authorities, the Papago once expressed the danger to land and life that the border's proximity created for them. Who was ultimately to be responsible for patrolling it and for protecting residents from damage? One by one, the government agencies replied in their best bureaucratic jargon that they each had partial jurisdiction, but that it was the duty of the "particulars" living along the border to maintain the fences and to keep "aliens" from illegally crossing onto their lands.

Isidro stood up and roared, "THEN IF IT IS UP TO US, WE WILL TEAR YOUR BORDER FENCE DOWN!"

After the resolutions passed, Isidro began to concentrate on the land rather than its legalities. To keep the right to land in

Mexico, you must work it. Land abandoned for more than two seasons can be claimed by squatters or *ejido* cooperatives, who can then stay on it as long as they use and improve it. While Isidro had been working in Arizona with resolutions and documents, he had been worried that his homestead might be confiscated, if not by Juan Stone, then by opportunistic *colonistas*. He has thus gone down every weekend, to plant fields and gardens when there was rain, to fix up the buildings and grounds when there wasn't.

The fruition of his wheat planting and the passing of the resolutions coincided. In *"gracias a Dios,"* he began planning for a feast in honor of San Isidro, the agricultural guardian and his patron saint. In early June I stopped by Isidro's place in Sells, but he was not there. Isidro had retired from his research and political activities in order to spend more time farming in Sonora.

The next time I saw Isidro, the talk was of *pinole*, not politics. We spoke too of the best time to plant beans and corn. "To me, the most beautiful thing is the coming of the first summer thunderstorms. I stay outside and watch the sky. I know it is time for things to grow again."

CHAPTER 6

Plants Which Coyote Steals, Spoils, and Shits On

We were picking watermelons all day, taking them to the shed
and stacking them. The next morning as the sun was coming, I
was just sitting there waking up, when I looked out and there
he was—Coyote—carrying away this watermelon. He was running along, carrying it between his front legs. I went over there
to the shed and all those melons were just about gone.

REMEDIO CRUZ, *BIG FIELDS*

Coyote—he's a hard one to write about and get away with it.

I tried once before. One winter, I went around to the villages
asking the Desert People about him. By the end of the cold season, I had a whole notebook full of stories.

The *old* stories. How, after the Flood, Elder Brother let Coyote help him make a new batch of people to start the world over
again. Coyote fooled around and made a bunch of misshapen
creatures, with eyes on their knees, with only one leg, or with
their sexual organs in the wrong places. Elder Brother just had to
throw them away, far across the ocean.

And dirty stories. Like the time he volunteered to carry a pretty
girl across a river, but told her to throw her skirts up over her eyes
so that they wouldn't get wet. Pretending to help her across, he
helped her get pregnant instead.

Yet nothing became of those stories I wrote down. It seemed I
had misplaced the notebook. For weeks, I searched without luck.

The following summer, I was walking near the village they call
Ban Dak, Where Coyote Sat Down, when I came upon a *charco*
that had just filled up with floodwaters. There, floating in the

pond, was a notebook that looked familiar to me, except it had pawprints smudging the pages, and whole sections ripped out by the teeth.

You have to watch what you say about this one they call Coyote.

For a long while, I wasn't sure of the difference between the legendary Coyote and the wild, dog-like critter I'd catch glimpses of out in the desert now and then. Is Coyote a special coyote? And if so, would I recognize him if I saw him up close? I spoke with trappers and zoologists, and memorized all the identifying features characteristic of ordinary coyotes. If I saw anything peculiar, then, I'd know who it was.

My time came one dusk as I was driving home to Esperero Canyon after a day of observing birds near Sonoita. Just as I pulled off the pavement onto the dirt road, I spotted a coyote up ahead of me. I braked the car, then glided slowly toward the middle of the road where he stood. He moved to the roadside on my left. I killed the engine.

He paused there for a moment, so I quickly grabbed the binoculars out of my knapsack, and took a good look at him: the pale pattern of fur around his neck; the hang of his tail; the taper of his snout; the shape of his eyes. He looked *muy típico*.

He stood there for a couple of minutes, still but attentive. Satisfied that he was just a plain old coyote, I finally put the binoculars down.

Then a funny thing happened.

He started to trot off, but stopped, and turned again toward me. Fixing his eyes on me, he slowly walked a complete ring around the car. When he had come full circle, he stopped, tossed his head back, and *yawned*, then walked off.

By the time it hit me that there's a little of Coyote in every coyote, I had realized that there's some Coyote in a lot of humans too.

The Desert Smells Like Rain

That wasn't news to my Papago friends—their stories are full of Coyotes in men's clothing.

Ban—coyote and Coyote go by the same simple name in the Papago tongue. The Papago call the legendary Coyote by laudatory euphemisms in certain tales—Our Furry Friend, Gray Partner, Burning-Eyed Buddy—but most of the time the word *Ban* does the trick. On the other hand, there is a rich array of words to describe not-so-praiseworthy Coyote-like attributes in humans (or vice versa). Linguist Madeline Mathiot put a few of them into print before Coyote could swipe her notebook.

Bankaj refers to any coyote-like quality, such as "yelling like a coyote." *Banma* describes one who is being greedy. *Banmad* is a verb meaning "to cheat somebody." *Banmakam* is a glutton. *S-banow* is the superlative for the bad breath of someone who "sure stinks like a coyote."

The name for a Pulaski is *ban wuhioṣa*—Coyote's face. Every time I ask a friend why those tools are called that, he breaks out laughing and says, "Well, don't they look just like me?" The *ban wuhioṣa* is the main tool used by the crew of "community beautifiers" that get paid by the government to keep the village clean of all weeds and debris. The nickname of the work crew?

Ba:ban-Pioñ—the Coyote Workers. The Papago phrase used for nicknames? *Ban'i kuadc*—"Coyote peeked in."

My first lesson about Coyote's plants left a bad taste in my mouth, to say the least. I had brought some wild desert gourds out to a village with me, curious to find if the Papago used them in any way. An elderly woman looked at the little gourds in the bed of my pickup.

"What you got there? Oh, that's what they call *a:ḍ!* Long time ago they used to go out, and when those fruit got ripe and turned yellow, they would eat it just like a sweet apple."

Before she had a chance to finish her story, I grabbed one tender, yellow gourd and took a bite into it. She yelled "DON'T" but it was too late—that taste was so terrifically bitter that my tongue muscles went into shock. I spat the pulp out and ran for water.

When I returned to where the woman was, she was grinning.

"It *used* to taste just like an apple, they say. Then Coyote came along and he *shit* on it. I guess ever since then it has had that taste that is in your mouth right now. . . ."

Over the next couple of years, I learned a lot about the two gourd species that different Papago refer to as *a:ḍ—Cucurbita foetidissima*, and *Apodanthera undulata*. In Spanish as well as English, these gourds are called coyote melons. Both contain bitter substances called *cucurbitacins*, that are found in all of the wild relatives of cultivated squashes and pumpkins. In fact, an important change during the evolution of domesticated squashes was the loss of bitterness in the fruit. Some ancient Indian probably tasted an ancient gourd and discovered a mutant that was *not* bitter! That was fortunate for him, and fortunate for us too—the seeds of it that he saved and grew were the start of a line of sweet-tasting fruit. All squashes with edible pulp have been derived from a few rare mutants found by chance. Prior to that, gourd-like squashes and pumpkins were grown primarily for their edible seed and the containers that could be made from their hard rinds.

A few months after I had the Coyote taste-test, I told the story to Don Bahr, who was deeply involved in learning Pima and Papago songs at the time. "Oh, there are a number of songs and legends referring to plants that are specifically named Coyote's this or that. You should find out about the other ones too."

So I did. And while Coyote hadn't exactly dumped on all of them, he hadn't left any of them in very good shape either. There was *Ban Tokĭ*, or Coyote Cotton, which grows in the canyons of the Baboquivaris, and occasionally in Papago fields.

Its leaves and flowers look like regular cotton, but the bolls lack a crucial ingredient—spinnable lint. Thanks to Coyote, they got the short end of the deal when it came to cotton fiber and are worthless to weavers.

Then there's *Ban Bawĭ*—Coyote Tepary Beans. They, too, frequent canyons, sometimes twining around the stems of Coyote Cotton. The Papago used to try harvesting them, but it became too much work—the seeds explode out of the ripe pods when you touch them, scattering over the ground. You could harvest them by picking them up if they were easy to see like the big white and red-brown domesticated teparies that Papago grow in their fields. But no, the Coyote Teparies look just like gravel, and are easily lost in the shuffle. Today Papago only grow the larger, brighter-colored tepary bean varieties, having given up the wild harvest by the late 1940s.

The kicker for me was in finding out about *Ban I'hug-ga*, or Coyote's Devil's Claw. Because its yellow flower is shaped like a shoe, one wild devil's claw species is also called *Ban Ṣu:ṣk*, meaning Coyote shoe, sandal, or tire. Another species of devil's claw has been cultivated by the Papago for the fiber produced from its dry, bony capsule—these black fibrous strips are woven into patterns in yucca and beargrass baskets that Papago women make.

The interesting thing is that botanists have been arguing for years as to whether or not the Papago had genetically altered the wild annual devil's claw species into a truly domesticated plant. This domesticated *I'hug* has longer fibers, pale flowers, and white (instead of black) seeds that germinate more quickly. Papago folk taxonomy clearly treats wild devil's claw species just as it does the wild relatives of other domesticated plants.

"Those other ones are *Ban I'hug-ga* because Coyote left them out in the desert. Now they are no good for making baskets with—those fibers are too small, too brittle. They just snap. You can't make anything out of them."

On a sunny winter day a Papago elder from Topowa sat with me in her field and told me the story of Coyote's Devil's Claw.

Both wild plants such as acorns and gourds and cultivated plants such as tepary beans and devil's claw are used by the Papago.

"One day Coyote was walking all over the desert, trying to find something to eat. He couldn't find anything, and he was too lazy to grow anything himself. So he walked and walked until he found what looked like a bone in the sand.

"He tasted it. It had no taste. It was too dry. So he sat down, thinking. Then he started to jump up and down, yelling, 'I think this bone wants to tell me that I will find something to eat around here.'

"So he ran around. All he saw was desert, no food. Then he came to a wide wash. He tried to jump across, but he landed in the middle of it, on top of a little green plant half buried in the sand.

"'This looks like it would be good to eat,' Coyote said, and he gobbled down the whole plant—root, bony fruit, seeds, and all.

"Glad that he didn't have to work to get his food, he decided to lie down and sleep. But after a while, he woke up with a big pain in his stomach. He got so sick that he had to get the plant out of his insides. He buried it in the sand and hoped he would not see it again. 'They don't like me and I don't like them.'

"But each year when the rain comes, those plants come up again. The floods carry the bony fruit and bury more of them in the sand where they can grow. Pretty soon, Coyote sees those plants he doesn't like all around. When the Desert People learn that they make him sick, they decide to say it is his plant. His devil's claw. *Ban I'hug-ga.*"

Around 1911, Papago Juan Dolores recorded the story of a time when Coyote *did* try to grow his own food. Well, sort of, in a way. He was given some good corn seed after the fall harvest, but instead of saving it for the next planting, he ate nearly all of it. When the summer rains finally came, he had forgotten to prepare some good land. He finally just threw the seeds along the bad ground around a wash.

Then Coyote slept through the growing season. He didn't learn the right songs to sing to the corn when it did come up. Knowing that he had to sing something to make it grow, he just made up a song. It was terrible.

The corn grew anyway. But it didn't grow up to be corn, because it never heard the corn's songs. In a poor place like the rough edge of a wash, only another kind of plant would grow. The plants grew up to be *Ban Wiw-ga*, Coyote's Tobacco.

Another time, Coyote stole real tobacco for his own. Real tobacco was grown in secret places. If a man other than its keeper saw it sprouting, the plant would sink into the ground. It was used in the sacred smoke houses by tribesmen, and could bring enlightenment: the ability to see in the dark, to talk with the dead, to sense the source of a companion's disease, and to realize its cure.

Coyote saw this magic plant where it sprouted from the grave of a powerful woman. Before anyone could stop him, the Furry Thief ran along, snatched some up, and went into the Smoke House as if he had some business there. He rolled himself a cigarette, then smoked it by himself, not even passing it around. It didn't matter. By that time it was Coyote's Tobacco, and wasn't too good for curing and seeing. He just saw the world like he always did. Like a Coyote.

Nearly all Coyote's plants are closely related to domesticated crops, seeds which the Papago say they have grown "since the beginning." These wild seedstocks, as Coyote's plants, are considered by Papago to be genetic retrogrades rather than possible progenitors of the crops. This is because Papago life *prior to* having these cultivated crops is now unthinkable; without these domesticated plants, their culture would not exist in the way it has for centuries. Hence, these wild plants associated with Coyote must be degenerated from their original, useful forms. It's as if Coyote snatched sweet apples from a Papago Garden of Eden, only to watch them turn sour and shriveled.

In contrasting Coyote's plants with *O'odham* domestic plants, Papago storytellers are making their people aware of two matters: that these plants are, in fact, related; and that they should do their best to care for and improve the quality of their crops, lest they deteriorate into less useful forms.

But it turns out that these wild relatives of crops *aren't* worth less; it has simply taken scientists time to recognize their relatedness to crops, and how to make use of it. Plant breeders are now using such wild relatives to improve the crops in our fields and protect them from pestilence. For it has been discovered that Coyote's plants are often hardy and resistant.

In the 1940s, plant breeders used wild Arizona cotton in a triple hybrid including cultivated upland cotton. They found a Coyote trick hidden therein. Although wild cotton is nearly lintless, its genes contributed fiber strength to cultivated upland cotton. Thus a better-quality cotton for weaving was developed using a plant that was "worthless" to weavers. Hybrids which included these wild cotton genes were also found to have pink boll worm resistance.

More recently, scientists have attempted to transfer other wild cotton genes to cultivated varieties to diminish the size of the bracts surrounding their flowers. In cotton processing, these bracts crumble into dust-like particles which have in the past been a cause of respiratory disease among workers.

For years, scientists have been interested in transferring the heat, drought, and blight resistance of tepary beans to other kinds of cultivated beans. Crosses between teparies and Great Northerns have been made, but always with considerable difficulty. Dr. Howard Scott Gentry, who made many collections of wild beans over the last half century, then suggested that these wild relatives should be used as "genetic bridges" to facilitate easier crosses between more distantly related cultivated varieties.

At Riverside, California, Claire Thomas and Giles Waines have recently had some success with this approach. By crossing cultivated teparies with Coyote's teparies, and doing the same with wild and domesticated common beans, they built a "bean bridge." These two hybrids can then be crossed with less difficulty, resulting in the transfer of tepary genes to other beans.

Wild cucurbits are now being used to improve the disease resistance of squashes. Collections of Coyote-like gourd species from Mexico have proved to have high levels of resistance to powdery mildew and to certain cucumber and watermelon mosaic viruses.

So I wonder what other tricks Coyote is preparing. Year after year, he steals watermelons from my Papago friends and goes down to hide them in the wash. He eats the big, cool fruit, spitting and shitting out the seed. Now and then, downstream from villages, I see small, ugly watermelons growing by themselves in the dry wash. What has he done to them? How bad do they taste?

CHAPTER 7

Where the Birds Are Our Friends

The Tale of Two Oases

In this lake there lived a monster, much larger than a man, who hated people, and killed them when they came for water.

THE MONSTER OF QUITOVAC

A cloudless sky, a bone-dry road. After miles of eating dust on a drive parallel to the border, we had arrived at what seemed an apparition—a little pocket of greenery in an otherwise harsh grey habitat.

Soon my old Papago friend Remedio had found his way down the trail to the pond. The next thing I knew, he was crawling on his hands and knees out onto the trunk of a cottonwood tree that reached over the water. He hung one arm down and scooped up a drink.

"Sure is *sweet* water. What do they call this place?"

"Depends on who you talk to," I mumbled, glancing across at an Organ Pipe Cactus National Monument placard. "Well, the Park Service calls it Quitobaquito, after the Mexican *Quitova-quita*. And three hundred years ago, Padre Kino christened it *San Seguio*. But all I ever heard your people call it is *A'al Waipia*."

"A'AL WAIPIA? This is it?" He was stunned for a moment. "In all of my life I never thought I would get to see this place where we are standing! I just thought we were going to another place because those signs didn't say *A'al Waipia*. So this is where those little waters come up from the ground!"

Those little springs, which the Papago call *ṣonagkam*, flow into a modest pond touted as one of the few authentic desert oases on the continent.

Out in a stretch of the Sonoran Desert where any sources of potable water are few and far between, *A'al Waipia* has been more than just a curious landmark. It is a critical *watermark* that has literally served and saved thousands of lives over the centuries.

Listen to the crusty explorer Carl Lumholtz soften under its touch around 1910:

> ... The little stream of crystal clear spring water at Quitovaquita is smaller than a brook, but it seemed much alive as it hurried on in its effort to keep the dam full. As I had been long unaccustomed to seeing running water, and for twenty days had drunk it more or less brackish, the tiny brook seemed almost unreal and was enchanting in its effect. It was also a delight to indulge in my first real wash for nine days.

Where a spring bubbles up in the desert, water-loving plants cuddle around it. Thus *A'al Waipia* has been an ecological oasis, a spot of lush riparian growth. As such, it attracts vagrant and migrant bird species from the seas, seldom seen in the arid interior.

And that's what the Park Service plays on—they offer us a cool, shady sanctuary where we can sit and watch birds, and ponder over a little pond filled with endangered desert pupfish.

But, unfortunately, *A'al Waipia* is no more than a shadow of what it once was. To sense its historic significance, one must go to another place. Off the beaten track. A true Sonoran oasis, thirty miles to the south of Organ Pipe Cactus National Monument, in old Mexico. *Ki:towak*.

My pickup truck bounced along over the washboard road. Amadeo, Remedio, and I pointed out plants to each other as we went—the bristle-topped senita cactus, heavy-trunked ironwood trees, and odorous, yellowish-green croton shrubs.

We edged over a rise, and all of a sudden the desert was whisked away—palms and cottonwoods reached above the horizon, and teal splashed up into the air. Amadeo grabbed his field glasses—a white-faced ibis down on the mudflats of the pond, and a couple of pigs foraging in the saltgrass.

Remedio sighed, knowing that this place was the place he had heard of: *"Ki:towak."*

We parked the pickup beneath a towering California palm; then Remedio and I walked over toward an old Papago house sitting almost on the edge of the pond. Amadeo took off in the other direction to survey birds—he would sight twice as many species that afternoon as we had seen at *A'al Waipia* in the morning.

A lean old Papago quietly greeted us as we approached his house made of saguaro ribs and organ pipes. Luis Nolia had been born nearby and was now the oldest living resident of the Papago settlement. A descendant of the semi-nomadic Sand Papago, he had as a child gathered the sweet underground stalks of sandfood in the dunes to the west, and eaten them like *carne machaca*. His family's women had crushed mesquite pods in bedrock mortars, and the men had transformed themselves into animals by wearing the fur masks and hoods of the *Wi'igita* ceremony.

Decades ago, Luis himself had been lured to the U.S. by wages to be earned picking cotton. After his wife died and his sons had grown up and settled in Arizona towns, he became lonely for the old ways and returned to Sonora. Now he grows summer field crops, keeps an orchard and a few animals, and is knowledgeable about the many medicinal plants with which the oasis springs are blessed.

Luis too blesses the oasis, for his work keeps it healthy. He is proud of the way the springs flow unencumbered by debris—he

The summer *Wi'igita* ceremony is performed today only by the Papago at *Ki:towak*.

has dug out the fallen sediment so that the streamlets run clear from their source. Every summer, Luis plants squash, watermelon, beans, and other vegetables. His plowing and irrigation encourage at least six species of wild greens which he harvests at various times. Various medicinal plants and Olney's tules (for which *Ki:towak* is named) grow in the irrigation ditches.

Luis is appreciative of trees, too, and his plantings literally rim the oasis and field edges of *Ki:towak*. The willow cuttings that he stuck into the pond bank grew quickly into saplings and now stabilize the earth. He harvests willow branches to make leafy crosses that hang on the walls of every Papago household at *Ki:towak*, but keeps his own supply alive. Elderberry, salt cedar, date, and California palm are planted near his house to provide shade. Wolfberry, mesquite, and palo verde form a hedge on his field edge, and thorny brush is piled between the shrubs to discourage stray cattle from entering.

He has dug fig and pomegranate shoots from the base of ancient, abundantly-bearing trees, and transplanted them out to more open areas in the orchard where they can thrive. He offered Remedio and me a bag of figs and a few white-seeded, rusty-shelled pomegranates to savor.

Earlier in the day, walking on the west side of *A'al Waipia*, Remedio and I came upon a sight that made him sick inside. There were fruit trees—or the remnants of them—still putting out a few leaves (but no fruit) in an overgrown mesquite bosque. At least five pomegranate shrubs were dead, and another eighteen were dying. Just a few rangy, unpruned figs were left.

"Poor things, such old trees left with no one to help them!" Remedio lamented. He wondered if they could be dug up and given to a family who would care for them.

They were a reminder that until 1957, *A'al Waipia* had been a *peopled* oasis just as *Ki:towak* is today. Looking down at the foot of the dying fruit trees, we saw irrigation ditches running along in much the same pattern as those which still function in the field/orchard at *Ki:towak*.

For *A'al Waipia* was formerly a Papago settlement too, with six-and-a-half acres of crops, and more of orchards.

Geographer Ronald Ives put it simply: "It is reasonable to believe that this settlement, situated at a perennial spring, has been continuously occupied since man came to the area."

The archaeological record bears out the suggestion of long inhabitance—seven distinct prehistoric and historic sites have been found on the U.S. side of the *A'al Waipia* area, and at least two major ones south of the border fence.

From the 1830s onward, there are records of the names of Papago inhabitants who lived at the oasis. After 1860, Mexicans and Americans came to stay at *A'al Waipia* too, some even intermarrying with the Sand Papago there. At least eight adobe houses were raised, a store and a mill were built, the pond deepened, and the ditches improved. But while visitors and buildings came and went, two Papago were patriarchs of the place for well over a century: Juan José and José Juan Orosco.

Juan José lived at the springs off and on from the 1860s until at least 1910, when Carl Lumholtz reported that he was well over a hundred but still in command of his faculties. José Juan Orosco, famous both as a medicine man and hunter, followed the older man as patriarch of *A'al Waipia* for several more decades. After Organ Pipe Cactus National Monument was established in 1937, Orosco's grazing rights were recognized, and he used them until his death in 1945.

The Park Service and the Papago disagree about what happened after that. The more-or-less official story is that José Juan Orosco's son Jim agreed to let the Park Service "condemn" his holdings in Organ Pipe Cactus National Monument, including "his" place at *A'al Waipia*. In return for the land and improvements he claimed by way of squatter's rights, Jim Orosco was given $13,000.

Some of the Papago tell versions of an altogether different story. One version claims that Jim Orosco never actually had exclusive rights to the place; he simply stayed there with the real caretaker, an old man called *S-Iawuis Wo:da*—'Worn Out Boot'—who was being paid by descendants of Juan José. The tellers of this version insist that *A'al Waipia* wasn't Jim Orosco's to sell: legally, all descendants of the two patriarchs should have been consulted. A great-granddaughter of Juan José lamented, "The old people knew it was wrong, but they didn't say too much when it happened."

Whether or not Jim Orosco could legally surrender Papago rights to *A'al Waipia*, it is clear that at the time the Park Service did not look upon the resident Papago as assets to the Monument. Orosco is reputed to have gone on drinking binges, and at one time, there was a Park Service sign on the road to the springs that said, "Watch Out for Deer, Cattle, and Indians."

The Papago farmland in the Monument was condemned without Congressional order, and without consultation with the Papago Tribe. By 1962, the National Park Service had destroyed all sixty-one structures remaining at *A'al Waipia* and the Growler Mine, wiping away most of the signs of human history in the Monument.

Bob Thomas of the *Arizona Republic* later commented on the Park Service's superficial commitment to its mandate of preserving ". . . various objects of historic and scientific interest." In a 1967 article entitled "Price of Progress Comes High," Thomas wrote:

> . . . Near Quitobaquito on the Organ Pipe National Monument a few years ago a government bulldozer knocked down the home of the late José Juan, a Papago Indian who lived there all his life. In doing so, workmen churned up the only known stratification of human habitation between Ajo and Yuma.

He added that the Papago:

... distrust the government's promises to protect the park's treasures. In the past, the government has unknowingly or unfeelingly destroyed historic and prehistoric artifacts in the area.

By this destruction, the Park Service gained a bird sanctuary to provide tourists with a glimpse of wild plants and animals that gather around a desert water source.

Or so they thought. For an odd thing is happening at their "natural" bird sanctuary. They are losing the heterogeneity of the habitat, and with it, the birds. The old trees are dying. Few new ones are being regenerated. There are only three cottonwoods left, and four willows. These riparian trees are essential for the breeding habitat of certain birds. Summer annual seedplants are conspicuously absent from the pond's surroundings. Without the soil disturbance associated with plowing and flood irrigation, these natural foods for birds and rodents no longer germinate.

Visiting *A'al Waipia* and *Ki:towak* on back-to-back days three times during one year, ornithologists accompanying me encountered more birds at the Papago village than at the "wildlife sanctuary." Overall, we identified more than sixty-five species at the Papago's *Ki:towak*, and less than thirty-two at the Park Service's *A'al Waipia*. As Dr. Amadeo Rea put it, "It is as if someone fired a shotgun just before we arrived there. The conspicuous absences were more revealing than what we actually encountered."

When I explained to Remedio that we were finding far fewer birds and plants at the uninhabited oasis, he grew introspective. Finally, the Papago farmer had to speak:

"I've been thinking over what you say about not so many birds living over there anymore. That's because those birds, they come where the people are. When the people live and work in a place, and plant their seeds and water their trees, the birds go live with them. They like those places, there's plenty to eat and that's when we are friends to them."

I think that Remedio would even argue that it is natural for birds to cluster at human habitations, around fields and fence rows. I'll go even further. It's in a sense natural for desert-dwelling humans over the centuries to have gathered around the *A'al Waipia* and *Ki:towak* oases. And although they didn't keep these places as pristine wilderness environments—an Anglo-American expectation of parks in the West—the Papago may have increased their biological diversity.

So if you're ever down in Organ Pipe Cactus National Monument and visit the Park Service wildlife sanctuary of Quitobaquito, remember that an old Papago place called *A'al Waipia* lies in ruin there. Its spirit is alive, less than forty miles away, in a true Sonoran Desert oasis. There, the irrigation ditches are filled with tules, and they radiate out from the pond into the fields like a green sunburst. *Ki:towak.*

CHAPTER 8

Gathering

We always kept gruel in our house. It was in a big clay pot that my mother had made. She ground up seeds into flour. Not wheat flour—we had no wheat. But all the wild seeds, the good pigweed and the wild grasses. . . . Oh, good that gruel was! I have never tasted anything like it. Wheat flour makes me sick. I think it has no strength. But when I am weak, when I am tired, my grandchildren make me a gruel out of the wild seeds. That is *food*.

CHONA, IN AUTOBIOGRAPHY OF A PAPAGO WOMAN

Today, all is not well among the Papago. Nutrition-related diseases virtually unknown in *Pimería Alta* a half century ago are taking their toll within the Papago and River Pima population. Nearly non-existent among Indians prior to 1940, diabetes and gall bladder disease have been affecting these Northern Pimans at an alarming rate since the mid-1950s. Today, more than half of all adult Papago suffer from these diseases. The prevalence of adult-onset diabetes among Northern Pimans is possibly the highest on the planet. More recently, the incidence of hypertension and heart disease has begun to rise. Both of these problems are known to have been *extremely* infrequent among the Papago before the 1950s. Since the 1940s, nurses routinely examining the skin, gums, tongues, lips, and eyes of Papago children have noted the physical effects of certain vitamin and mineral deficiencies. A Papago nurse grieved, "My people are just being wasted away by these diseases."

As I talked with Lusiano Dolores over a meal, the discussion turned to diabetes. What bothered him about the prevalence of this disease today is that it seemed to have come from no-where.

"Maybe it was the foods they ate, but the Old People never had sugar diabetes. Those people got to be real old too, some over a hundred, and they just kept on working. They didn't need any insulin or to have their legs cut off because the blood stopped reaching them. But now we wonder where this sickness came from all of a sudden, and can't figure it out. One man told me once that maybe they let some germs out during the World War that just floated through the air, and finally settled here, way down low in the desert where we live. I have thought about that, and other things, and I just don't know."

Doctors have yet to offer a clear explanation of why these nutrition-related diseases increased so suddenly. They note in passing that the Indian diet has changed for the worse, but what does that mean? Papago have readily accepted foreign foodstuffs such as beef, lard, melons, sugar, white flour, and coffee since the 1600s. It is simplistic to assume that any one of these foods is the cause of the problem, because all of them were introduced decades before the sharp rise in disease. Nor is it true that many Papago and Pima are obese and diabetes-prone because they consume inordinately more calories than the rest of us. An over-weight, diabetic *O'odham* adult can ingest a comparatively mod-est number of calories every day, yet maintain a weight of 200 to 300 pounds. Diet studies in the villages have indicated that the average *O'odham* today consumes about the same number of calories, and the same amounts of carbohydrates and fat, as the average U.S. citizen.

The real problem may just be that the Papago *do* eat like the average European-American. Their metabolism may be adapted to an altogether different diet. To understand the extent to which the modern American diet deviates from the traditional diet of the Papago, we must get a sense of the ecology of their native food resources.

"Oh, this little wild onion, *I'itoi siwol,* is that what you mean?" Lean old Casimiro Juan squinted at me, then off at the mountains. "Don't you know? You can't find those ones now, sometimes you can't even see them until it gets cold. They're still sleeping underground."

"Are they hard to find at the right time?" I asked.

"No, not if you know where to look," he laughed. "That's why I'll come with you and show you, but you gotta wait until it is the right time—You know, my brother who's not here anymore was the one who took me over there to *Waw Kiwulik* the first time to pick them. I had been hearing about those onions there, and he knew it, so he said, 'Well, get your horse and we'll go over there.'

"We were riding and I was looking up into the mountains wondering where those onions were hiding. We were in a big sandy wash just below the first rocks when my brother said, 'Look down around the horse.' Then I looked around on the ground and it was all covered with the *siwol* coming up.

"I got down off my horse and started to dig them out of the sand and put them into a big gunny sack. My brother went off to hunt for a while but pretty soon he came back. He started laughing. I said, 'Why you laughing so hard?' He said, 'Who gonna carry that gunny sack back home?' Then I looked at it and it was too full and heavy to even get on my little horse.

"That's when I knew I picked too many. So I just opened the bag and saved a bunch of big ones. Then I sat down and planted most of those onions I picked back in the sand so that they could grow again. When you take me there, I'll show you. They still keep coming up there."

Papago country consists of well over two and a half million acres in the heart of the Sonoran Desert. For at least 8,000 years it has supported people, first by food they gained from hunting and gathering, and later by domesticated as well as wild resources.

Spines are brushed off the young, tender flower buds of cholla cactus, a Papago delicacy.

Even in the driest pocket of North America—the Pinacate—Papago historically subsisted on legumes from hardy trees, lizards, bighorn, and a root parasite called sandfood. Occasionally, runoff from volcanic slopes was enough to produce a cultivated crop.

While the desert appears unproductive to most visitors from tropic or temperate zones, it served the Desert People well, given their population levels. There is reason to believe that during most years, the desert produced more food than could be harvested by local Papago villages. This includes greater quantities of favored foodstuffs than could be gathered even if the Desert People had the time: mesquite pods, palo verde and ironwood beans, saguaro seed and pulp, cholla cactus buds, prickly pear pads and fruit, greens, chia and tansy mustard seeds, rabbits, game birds, and underground stems, roots, and bulbs.

Some of these wild masts can fail with drought, or in years of late frost, but it is unlikely that all major food sources could be laid waste within the same year. Movement to other wild stands and barter with other villages also buffered Desert People from the effects of local fruit failure.

From recent analyses of desert food composition and yield in the wild, it appears that neither harvestable calories nor protein are limited in Papago country. Energy-rich carbohydrates were available in mesquite pod flour, seeds of winter ephemerals, saguaro and wolfberry fruit, and other locally abundant desert plants. In adjacent mountain ranges within a day's distance from some Papago villages, acorns, roots, and piñon nuts can be found. Add to that the variety of cultivated beans, squash, and grains grown by the Papago, and it is clear that their diet could also have been high in protein *quality*—there was enough overlap between the amino acids of various plant food sources to provide a complete protein when they were eaten together in the customary pattern.

Then what of vitamins and minerals? These are more inequitably distributed through the edible products of the plant kingdom. Yet the Sonoran Desert has such a diversity of lifeforms that fortunately a full range of nutrients can be found among its many productive species.

Nutritionist Ruth Greenhouse has recently discovered good to excellent sources of iron and calcium in many of the wild greens the *O'odham* gather. She also confirmed an earlier finding that the flower buds of cholla cactus, relished by Papago, contain more calcium in a four-ounce serving than there is in a glass of milk. Wolfberries and chiltepines, the wild perennial chile of the desert, are sources of considerable amounts of vitamins A, B2, and C. Saguaro, gourd, and devil's claw seeds are rich in edible oils that generally carry with them certain B vitamins. At particular times of the year, it appears that certain required nutrients were available in abundance.

This is not to say that historic Papago never exhibited the deficiency symptoms such as bleeding gums or loose teeth that nurses noted in the 1940s. In the old days, to be sure, there was much more variation than there is now in the availability of nutrients, both from season to season and from year to year.

Yet it is difficult to imagine a Papago with a vitamin C deficiency while living in a saguaro-harvesting camp, or lacking calcium for the weeks following a cholla bud pit roast. The same person, however, may show deficiency symptoms during the "lean months" of late winter before desert fruits reappear.

This seasonal flux in nutrient availability may be what best characterizes the traditional Papago diet. Except for a few easily stored mainstays such as mesquite pod flour, roasted corn, dried beans, and chiles, most foods were available only for brief periods each year.

There are historic accounts of the *O'odham* gorging themselves on saguaro fruit for weeks, gaining weight rapidly during that time. They then went back to their fields and sometimes lived on bloodroot amaranth greens until the crops ripened.

The Desert Smells Like Rain

Over an annual cycle, as many as six discrete pulses of wild foods can occur, each with its own complex of plant species that reach harvesting stage simultaneously. Because some of these wild foods do not lend themselves to long-term storage, the Desert People take advantage of them while available. They have relied on their own bodies to store this energy.

As another harvesting period rolled around, the people looked upon it as a blessing. As we were gathering greens one spring, an *O'odham* woman told me that "*Jewed Makai*, the Earth Maker, gave us different green things for each time of the year."

A harvest is also a welcome change of pace. "Oh, that was such a good time," Maggie laughed, recalling the acorn harvest up in the mountains near *Ali Wak*. "I guess it was like our vacation, getting away from our houses to go where it is cool. We went up to *Waik Wiyo:di* and all us ladies would just sit and talk and gather those *wiyo:di* all day long. It wasn't even like work. First we put the tarp on the ground and made one of the kids go up and shake the tree to get those acorns to fall. Then it rained hard and swept most of them away. So we just rolled up our pants to the knee and waded across the stream until we found a tree with some left hanging. We stayed in the shade all day, picking them one by one, like they were berries. . . . I don't even know how many we came home with, because we cracked them open as we picked them, and ate a lot right while we were there, before the bugs got into them."

The major change in the Papago diet over the last half century may be the demise of seasonality. Papago men who joined the Civilian Conservation Corps or military service in the thirties became accustomed to a "regular diet" of highly processed foods with long storage life. By the forties, government rations were introduced to the reservation as well. At the same time, many Papago abandoned their own farming and gathering activities to work for wages in irrigated cotton fields. The stores where they spent their wages for food had a limited number of foodstuffs, mostly white flour, pinto beans, coffee, salt, sugar, and other "staples." These became the cotton picker's diet *day after day*. In 1959, surplus commodity food distribution was a notable part of government aid to Indians. By 1968, the commodities distributed through the EFMS (Emergency Food and Medical Services) program had become the predominant food source for some Papago families, further reinforcing redundancy.

While some would argue that the program did bring enriched flour and fruit (canned) to people who desperately needed the nutrients that those foods contained, it is crucial nevertheless to know what these foods replaced. Dr. Doris Calloway and associates have shown that nearly all the commodity foods are lower in mineral and protein content than the counterpart foodstuffs that the Papago, Pima, and Hopi traditionally gathered or grew in their fields. It has also been speculated that these government-introduced foods have higher sodium chloride (salt) content than food previously available to Papago, a possible factor in the increase in hypertension. Historically, mineral salt was available only after pilgrimages to the Gulf of California, although consumption of plant ash, halophytic greens, and clay provided trace minerals at other times. It is also probable that the government-subsidized foods are lower in soluble fiber and favor faster digestion compared to traditional foods.

But the change in *kinds* of food was not all; equally important was the change from a seasonally responsive diet to one of year-round uniformity. The Papago metabolism may not be adapted to such uniformity, if National Institute of Health epidemiologists are right. They feel that the diabetes-prone metabolism of the Papago and Pima worked positively in the time when there were wide seasonal and annual variations in the availability of foods. Although food availability is said to have varied according to "a feast and famine pattern," implying complete food failure at times, it may have simply been that the Papago diet was relatively richer in energy foods in certain seasons, and poorer in calories during other seasons.

Dr. Peter Bennett has suggested that certain genetic traits of Papago and Pima may now be maladaptive:

> It has been suggested that this population has been subjected to alternating periods of feast and famine. Could it be that those who were genetically predisposed to develop diabetes survived because of their ability to store as much food as possible when the food was plentiful, enabling them to avoid starvation when serious periods of famine take place?

Those predisposed to diabetes did likely gain weight quickly, but when sugars or fats were out of season, rapid weight loss improved insulin secretion, and diabetic symptoms would vanish. But as the regularity of availability of such foods increased, diabetes has become more persistent. In sufferers of diabetes today, insulin is not being produced in the right amounts at the right time.

Bennett's associate, Dr. Roger Unger, likens this desert-adapted human metabolism to that of desert rodents. When rains produce an abundance of energy-rich seeds, desert rats eat until they become obese. The energy stored in body fat is used until the next rainy season.

"But if you put the desert rat in a cage," Dr. Unger says, "and give him plenty of food, he gets so fat he can barely move." And that, he thinks, is what the modern diet has done to the Papago.

It's hard to point to any one factor that can altogether reduce the vulnerability of Papago to the problems of diabetes. There has been some success in combining exercise and gradual diet change into weight control programs for obese *O'odham*, reducing the day-to-day risks of this disease. While some medical practitioners recommend that patients come into clinics for "starvation diets" to drastically reduce weight, others point out that the weight is frequently gained back as soon as the person returns to village life. Some Papago and Pima diabetics turn not to modern medicine for help, but to traditional curing. Papago women now buy medicinal plant packages reputed to cure diabetes from Mexican herbalists at the Magdalena fiesta each October.

On the other hand, what about more emphasis on *gathering*, seasonally responding to locally available fresh foods? These native foods have proved to be nutritious, and the outdoor exercise involved in collecting them would certainly be beneficial. In another vein, one study has shown that eating prickly pear pads, a traditional Papago food, can beneficially control blood sugar levels of diabetic Indians. While no one expects the Papago to return entirely to a hunting and gathering mode of existence, there is plenty of room for a resurgence of part-time native food collecting. And who would want to see the *O'odham* go any farther the *other* way, accepting a dull diet that makes them like the unhealthy, hopeless desert rats stuck in a medical researcher's cage?

CHAPTER 9

Given Over to Santos and Spices

Magdalena's Fiesta

I lost you in the carnival, at the Saint's Day Feast where everyone is eaten, lost you in the fireworks, the street fever, the
smoke ... you who gave yourself over to santos and spices, to
ancient prayer ...

CHASING MAGDALENA, 1976

As we walked along down the shaded lane next to a Mexican
farmer's irrigation ditch, it seemed for a while as if we were the
only pilgrims. Dense hedges of elderberry, carrizo cane, and
vine-covered mesquite sheltered us from the sun's glare.

For the last hour, there had been only eight of us in sight. Carlos, the limping mineworker from Cananea, who had walked
for two days to fulfill his *manda*, a secret vow to San Francisco.
Two teenage Chicanas from Phoenix, whose fancy shoes had lost
their heels. Three Papago who kept together: Justicia, a plump
lady from *Ak-ciñ*, and her two middle-aged nephews. They had
walked along the Rio Magdalena floodplain from Imuris, where
Justicia's legs had given out on her last year. My wife and I had
been walking and talking with her from San Ignacio, just four
miles back. She was telling us how her family used to come by
wagon all the way from *Ak-ciñ*, for centuries before the government prohibited horses from crossing the border.

Then the lane turned, and at once we were out of the shade
with an open view to the south. We could see other pilgrims,
up on the highway shoulder, over on the railroad tracks, mov-

ing toward the same center. There in front of us was the town of Magdalena de Kino, shrouded by the wood smoke of scores of cooking fires.

Justicia stopped and silently crossed herself. As our conversation ceased, we could suddenly hear the fiesta, still more than a mile and a half away. The sound itself, muffled by the distance, was startling: more like a deep rumbling from the belly of the desert valley than anything humans could make. Yet it was the sound of ten thousand people celebrating in at least five languages, accompanied by a dozen *mariachi* and *norteño* bands, several hawkers amplified over blaring loudspeakers, and a number of squeaking, screeching carnival rides. In sum, it was the call of the Feast of St. Francis.

For over two centuries, Sonoran Desert dwellers have received strength from a reclining statue of Saint Francis kept in the church of Magdalena de Kino, Sonora. This San Francisco has become more than a saint to Sonoran Catholics—he embodies their mixture of native beliefs and the Hispanic Christianity that was brought to them in the 1600s. In fact, some Papago believe that San Francisco and Padre Kino, the first Jesuit missionary among them, whose bones are now enshrined in Magdalena, are one and the same. Certain elders tell stories of San Francisco's coming alive and sitting up or weeping when Papago worshippers have visited him. Others say that he once carried an Indian bow, and that he has appeared in Papago villages. Though each Papago may have his own patron saint, San Francisco is still the crucial connection between the Papago People and the *Santu Himdag*, the Sacred Way.

Outsiders have puzzled over the fact that the pilgrims revere an image of San Francisco Xavier on the October fourth feast day of St. Francis of Assisi. Folk historian Jim Griffith observed that this paradox "is another relic of the confusion which attended the replacement of the Jesuits by the Franciscans two hundred years ago." Sonoran Indians were originally introduced to St. Francis Xavier by the Jesuits before that order was expelled from Sonora in 1767. The Papago must have assumed that the St. Francis of Assisi whom the new Franciscan priests spoke of was the same fellow.

With attributes of Xavier, Assisi, and Padre Kino welded into one image, the saint in Magdalena is certainly a powerful figure for the Papago. They visit him—to ask or thank him for his help, and to let him recharge the religious objects they have brought from home. If he has answered their prayers, their *mandas* to visit him must be met within a given period of time or else he will "send the bill back with calamities," as one Mexican observed.

Justicia had been working off her *manda* for two years. If St. Francis would help her brother regain the use of his arthritic arm, she had vowed to walk from Nogales clear to Magdalena. As she saw some signs of improvement in the arm, she began the walk from the border last year. Yet the journey proved to be too much for her—relatives found her collapsed near Imuris and took her back home. This year, she was determined to walk the rest of the way, despite the discouraging words of a new priest who had recently been assigned to her village.

"He said that the Indians don't understand about the religion, that if they just ask forgiveness of their sins they will be forgiven and they won't have to do penance and walk until they fall down. But I'm not doing it as a *punishment*, I'm walking to give thanks for the help that has come to my brother."

As we entered the plaza surrounding the cathedral, Justicia gave me two dollars to buy a *milagro*—a little copper effigy or *ex-voto*, in this case, of an arm. I brought it to where she stood in line outside the catafalque in which San Francisco rests. Upon reaching the door, she crossed herself, dropped to her knees, and moved toward him. Everyone gathered around the child-size statue, cradling him, thanking him, and saying silent prayers. Justicia pinned the *milagro* to his brown Franciscan habit and stayed with him for a few minutes more after the rest of us left.

As we departed from the cathedral, we noticed that a Yaqui deer dancer and a *pascola* were preparing to dance. The *pascola*, a thin, elderly man, had his goat hair and cottonwood mask looped to the side of his head—he was joking in a high-pitched voice, trying to make the deer smile, a feat that could never be accomplished. Justicia's nephews watched, amused for a while, but their thirst and hunger got the best of them. They went off to *Calle Libertad*, the "Papago alley," to buy a few beers and some fresh corn on the cob, then to gawk at the carnival freaks, transvestites, and *putas*. By the time we caught up with them, they were feeling no pain.

Dr. Henry Dobyns, the foremost historian of the Magdalena event for over three decades, has found evidence that Papago and Pima Indians originally held a harvest festival in early October, onto which the missionaries simply grafted a few Christian motifs. Though few live in the area today, the Rio Magdalena was once farmed by Imuris Pima. The harvest is still ingrained in the Magdalena monstrosity—pick-ups and wagons full of corn, red chiles, striped squash, and quinces roll into town to dazzle the pilgrims. As soon as the farmers sell their produce, they immediately buy other merchandise: saddles from local *talabarterias*; double-weave palm cowboy hats from Nacori Grande in the Sierra; Mayo rugs and baskets from the lowlands; synthetic blankets and cowboy shirts from bordertown *fabricas*; and *huaraches* from central Mexico. Booths displaying trinkets, hardware, religious paraphernalia, and food line the streets. Some foods, like barrel cactus candy, are local specialties. Others, such as cakes of popped amaranth seeds called *alegrías*, reach no further north from the Mexico City sources than this fiesta.

While the presence of so many tradesmen seems to shock visitors who expect a purely religious experience, this again is an

The Desert Smells Like Rain

unwieldy outgrowth of an ancient connection. Prehistoric trade routes connected the Indian tribes of what is now the Southwest of the United States with the great civilizations of Mesoamerica. Turkeys, crop seeds, precious stones, and medicines were distributed via a trade network linking cultures that lived thousands of miles apart. Historically, Sonoran Desert tribes participated in a more localized network that spanned the present international border—Papago and Pima baskets were traded southward; chiles, macaws, and sea shells were exchanged northward.

No doubt intercultural trade has long been an established part of the Magdalena festival. Since the 1840s, according to Dobyns, "a fully developed secular fair was held each fall in connection with the cult pilgrimage of St. Francis Xavier." For decades, Opata, Yaqui, Mayo, and River Pima have mingled with the Papago at the fiesta. Today you may even see Cora from Nayarit and a few Navajo from northern Arizona.

Though most of the items sold at the fiesta are of modern manufacture, unheard of a century ago, some things are unchanged. Medicinal herbs and agricultural produce are the organic threads that tie today's trade to that of the past.

Medical anthropologist Margarita Kay feels that, at Magdalena, these complement San Francisco's power of healing:

> Such church fiestas are common throughout Mexico, but the one for St. Francis has a unique emphasis on curing. This stress is demonstrated by the extensive commerce in folk medicine visible at the fiestas. There are many stalls for merchants of herbs who come from all over Sonora and from as far away as Veracruz....

Some of the native herbal medicines sold at Magdalena today are among those described by the first missionaries arriving in Sonora: *cocolmeca*, a diuretic, also used for menstrual difficulties; *jojoba*, for sores and burns; *yerba colorada*, for tonsil infections and coughs; *yerba del manzo*, for fevers and sore throats;

hediondilla, an emetic, or a poultice for rheumatism; and *chuchupate,* for colds. All these native herbs, and introduced ones such as *manzanilla,* are used by the Papago. Because several of these are plants that grow only in moist places, the fiesta provides one of the few opportunities the Desert People have to replenish their medicine cabinets.

Justicia, having already visited San Francisco and treated herself to a beer, was ready to go shopping. She drafted my wife and me as guides and translators. Her nephews were still nowhere to be seen. She bought a cotton print scarf, a postcard of San Francisco, and a tequila bottle full of pickled green *chiltepines.* Then Justicia led us over to a Mexican herbalist. This widow from Bacadehuachi, Sonora, displayed her hand-gathered herbs on several blankets and baskets she had carried in with her. Laid out together in little piles, the roots, stems, and fruits looked exotic, despite the fact that many were common desert plants. Justicia became confused.

"Now that I see *all* those roots together, I'm not sure which one *we* use. And I don't know what its name is in *Jujkam ñeok.*"

My wife and I looked at each other. Swell, I thought. The herbalist knows only its Spanish name; Justicia knows only its Papago name; and all we know are the scientific names in Latin. So much for cross-cultural exchange.

Justicia was still frowning when Karen realized that herbs have ways of identifying themselves. "Well, Justicia, where does it grow? What is it good for?"

"*Hedai? Wa:wisa?* I used to get it from a man who dug it up at the springs and ditches around *Ki:towak* and *A'al Waipia.* It just grows where it's wet. Its root is good for sore throats, and some people use the leaves. I think they make you throw up."

Karen and I translated this into Spanish for the herbalist from Bacadehuachi. She listened, then immediately picked up a bunch of *yerba del manzo* roots. "*¿Este es?*"

Justicia took a good look at the roots, and tasted a fiber of one. "*Wa:wisa*—this is the one!"

When we finally came upon Justicia's nephews again, they were at the open-air dance hall and *cantina* where most Papago convene on *Calle Libertad*. A *mariachi* band with trombones, trumpets, and violins was blasting out a tune a few feet from where the older nephew was sleeping. He was still holding a bottle of *bacanora* in his hand. The other nephew had his hat on backwards and was dancing with a broom in the middle of the floor. Justicia giggled.

"We should have bought some *ku:la* [cures] for them—they're gonna feel sick tomorrow."

Yet in a way, the fiesta itself is a cure. For a brief period each year, the Papago leave their villages and many of their social constraints behind. Magdalena has an element of pandemonium to it, despite the fact that it is a patterned event. Daily routines are suspended. Many see this time as a relief from the monotony of jobs which they must endure the rest of the year. As such, no matter how tired and tipsy they get, the whole fiesta is recollected as a ritual of renewal. It alters their perception of things enough to give them a fresh start when they return home. Considering the number of people packed into two small plazas for four to six days, accidents and violence are remarkably infrequent. Its chaos somehow *works*.

Another band came into the hall and began to play the kind of borderlands polka that Papago love. Justicia gave Karen her packages and draped her purse-strap over her arm.

"You know how to polka?" she said to me. "Not like those *Milga:n* do, jumping up in the air! I mean the *O'odham* way to do it, where you stay on the ground! Come on, I'll show you so you can teach your wife. That's what they call *chicken-scratch!*"

Before I knew it, we had scratched the night away. A local rooster was crowing up the dawn.

CHAPTER 10

You Make the Earth Good
by Your Work

The desert is still their home. To most of them, it is still important whether rain comes or not. On the Reservation or off of it,
they watch carefully the fleeting clouds and are worried and
restless when no rain falls, when the desert will begin to look
brown, when seeds will lie dormant under the soil or unused
in the storehouses.

ROSAMUND SPICER, 1943

Remedio was leaning on his shovel, looking out over the desert,
talking to me as if he were *listening* for the things he wanted to
say, for the meaning to rise out of the desert and come to him.

"I have been thinking about this many nights now, about when
I leave here and go, no more on this earth, that I should begin to
prepare for that. And that's why I'm working today, to make a
new field and a shrine nearby. See, my mind has been going this
way, that I should be planting things. Leaving little green things
growing up, and gathering beautiful rocks from the desert for a
shrine to the saint who has taken care of me. *That's* how I want
to be remembered by my grandchildren, for the live things that
will just keep growing."

We were working on a new field for Remedio, digging a *charco*
and ditches to bring water from the wash to the new area he
wanted to plant. Remedio, who is now in his sixties, had to give
up his old floodwater field two years ago, after a government
flood control project cut off his source of stormwaters. He had
grown edgy after that, because he felt unable to fulfill his respon-

sibility as a *Tohono O'odham* to tend the earth and help the desert yield its food.

Then a dream came three weeks ago.

"There was my father in a far-off place, offering me some food. When you have a dream like that, and you take the food from someone you knew who is gone, you will be going their way in not too long. That is why I want to fix up this dirt, to make it good for the crops, so that those who live here after me will be able to grow what they need to eat *here* in this place."

That day, Remedio neither planted seeds nor gathered rocks. He simply worked the soil, preparing it for what would come later. His goal was to make *s-kegac jewed*—good earth.

Desert soils are characteristically poor in what agricultural plants need. They are low in organic matter, have poorly developed crumb structure, are patchy in their distribution of nitrogen and other nutrients, and tend to be so alkaline that certain nutrients aren't readily available to plant roots.

Down on one knee, working a handful of dirt through his fingers, Remedio acknowledged what he was up against.

"Too much *wepegĭ bid* (red clay) in that corner over there and a little too sandy here on this side," he says. "But if I can mix the different kinds of dirt together, and plow in some mesquite leaves and cow droppings, that *jewed* will get more and more soft and moist. If I can just work those things in, then maybe the dirt will get better."

Early references to Papago agriculture hardly mention any native concepts or methods of soil renewal. The presumption was that until Spaniards introduced plowing and manuring, the Desert People's only soil modification technology was the digging stick.

Sensing that other outsiders may have overlooked certain indigenous practices, anthropologist Cynthia Anson and I began to ask Papago farmers a simple question:

The Desert Smells Like Rain

"What makes the *jeweḍ* good in your field?"

We gradually accumulated notes on a considerable variety of soil modification methods, some of which could *not* have been introduced by the Spaniards. Even the introduced concept of manuring has taken a native turn on the Reservation—guano from desert bats is gathered from churches and mountain caves, and is spread in fields.

Yet far more interesting than manure is the use of other local materials: flood and firewood detritus, ash, crop wastes, and the litter beneath leguminous desert trees. The humus developed in association with tree legumes is a remarkable choice for soil amendments. Mesquite and ironwood are key in the nutrient balance of desert washes, since they may both pump and fix nitrogen that can then become available to aid in the growth of other plants. Papago families still seek out places where moist, rich litter has accumulated under these woody legumes, sensing what scientists have only recently confirmed. They then dig up the top two or three feet of organic matter around the trees, and take it back to their plants to enrich them.

The most important soil amendment for Papago fields is not something the People themselves carry into the fields—they merely encourage floods to haul it in. By properly locating their fields "at the mouths of washes," and by constructing low, water-spreading fences of woven brush, they help floodwater to dump its load of debris within the fields. Drifts of this material, called *wako'ola*, are left behind the water-spreaders after the flood has moved on.

Rummaging through a foot-high drift of *wako'ola* that had been deposited on a field near Topowa, I was surprised at the organic richness of its contents: rodent dung, mesquite leaves, mulch developed under trees, and water-smoothed twigs. The farmers at Topowa take this flotsam, spread it, and plow it into their soil. Enough of this humus comes into their fields to add an inch of organic matter to the cultivated surface each growing

A small *charco* pond filled with nutrient-rich floodwaters from the Baboquivaris.

season, reducing soil alkalinity and increasing moisture-holding capacity.

The significance of this technique is obscure until one realizes how typically impoverished desert soils are in organic matter. Remedio's new field, before it had even been worked, had an organic content of less than one half of one percent, and this is typical of arid lands. The Topowa field, having gathered flood detritus and drift for at least a century, had an organic content of five percent, comparable to that of good Grain Belt soil. And whereas Midwestern farmlands are annually losing forty or fifty tons of topsoil per acre and millions of dollars worth of nutrients to erosion, some Papago fields are gaining good soil.

One summer afternoon in Topowa, a sudden downpour hit the town just as I had crossed the big wash. Stranded for a while, I began to watch the water dance across the ground and accumulate down in the streambed. As I saw a frothy head develop on the moving water, it hit me that I had a few jars with me—why not run out and sample the *wako'ola* and the water itself? Jumping out of the pickup, I scrambled down to a small side channel that heads toward a friend's field and scooped up a jarful of the floating detritus, and another of the moving water in the channel.

An even more intense cloudburst roared up, and I ran back to the pickup, drenched. I watched the wash flow full-force for another ten minutes. Coors bottles, branches, and hubcaps floated by. Pillow-sized lumps of foam accumulated in the low branches of trees lining the streambank, then broke away and floated downstream—a sure sign that nutrients, as well as water, were charging toward my friend's field.

The jars made their way back to a lab in Tucson, and the results of tests were not too surprising. The running water itself did hold a modest amount of nutrients in soluble or suspended form, but the floating detritus was the "cream" of the stream. This flood-borne debris contained over fifty times as much nitrogen as the floodwater itself.

Desert ecologists tell us that aside from water, nitrogen is the most limiting factor for plant growth in arid lands. The elegance of Papago runoff farming is that when a field receives a fresh flush of water, it is simultaneously being recharged with nitrogen. A surge of crop growth is the inevitable result.

In 1917, H. V. Clotts finished an evaluation of the potential for further irrigation in Papago country. After noting that few of the desert villages had extensive irrigation systems, he had turned his attention to the ingenious ways the Indians gathered and utilized local, temporary surface runoff. He ended up visiting hundreds of Papago fields and dismissing altogether the idea of large irrigation projects to develop Papago country:

> The Papago Indians, by several hundred years of desert experience, are thoroughly conversant with the conditions in their country, and with consummate judgment have so located their charcos and fields as to secure maximum results from the limited rainfall available. We cannot go into their country with the idea of teaching them farming or irrigation under conditions as we find them in other parts of the country. Any attempt to introduce modern farming methods, as we understand them elsewhere, would result in disaster. The most we should do for these people is first to protect them in the possession of the land which they have beneficially used for hundreds of years. They should also have educational facilities and such modern agricultural machinery as would be adaptable, with some assistance in improving the stock industry. It is quite probable that they could be aided in the conservation of their very limited water. . . . If thus protected and left in peace they are fully capable of working out their own salvation, indeed they are particularly ambitious to do so. . . .

The latest controversy regarding the huge Central Arizona Project (CAP) is not *whether* irrigation water will be made available to the Indian tribes, but what they will do with it when it arrives. For years, southern Arizona Indians have been told that they will get a cut of the irrigation water that will be pumped uphill 300 miles from the Colorado River. This "cut" is presumably in exchange for the surface and groundwater that has been plundered from the tribes by their Anglo neighbors.

If Indian "involvement" in present irrigation projects indicates anything, it is that Indians will not necessarily be using the water allocated to them. For instance, between a half and a third of the San Carlos Irrigation Project water that arrives on the Gila River Indian Reservation is used by non-Indians who are leasing Pima and Maricopa lands. Because of the high alkalinity of this water, much of this leased land is being "salted up," and within a few years it develops an alkali crust that may make it worthless for crop production.

There are some who suggest that the tribes will never see most of their CAP allotments reach the reservations—the water will be sold to burgeoning cities, and the money will go into tribal coffers. Yet if the "gift" of CAP ever reaches the Papago Reservation, what will keep it from causing the disaster that H. V. Clotts anticipated a half century ago? Could it be that large-scale agricultural leasing will come to Papago country too, and that instead of the land being protected, it will be wasted? What then will happen to the Old Ways of the Desert People?

I asked Remedio what he thought of all the tribal meetings going on regarding plans for the CAP water. He laughed, tossing down his shovel.

"Yeah, I've been hearing about that water coming from the Colorado River ever since the 1930s and I still haven't seen it. When things like that are given to us, the government tells our People, 'Here you go, it's free.' But then we have to pay for getting it here and then for fixing things up when they break.

"Yeah, maybe some day when that water comes we will all be like the *Milga:n* then. We can have swimming pools and a big golf course with nothing on it.

"But since I can't swim, and I would probably club my foot instead of that little white ball if I tried, I hope I'm already gone when that Colorado River water comes. . . ."

He looked up into the skies above the Baboquivaris, then picked up his shovel again.

"Come on, my friend. We better get to work. It looks like maybe it's going to rain today, if we are lucky."

Notes

There are many students of the desert and Papago culture who have gone before me, and I have learned from them as well as from many good people on the reservation and in northern Mexico. These notes are designed to acquaint readers with the literature I have quoted and drawn upon, and to present more technical observations that friends and I have made in the field. All Papago words are written in the orthography formally supported by the tribe, and first published by Albert Alvarez and Kenneth Hale, "Toward a Manual of Papago Grammar," *International Journal of Linguistics* 36:2 (1970), 83–97. As noted in Acknowledgments, nearly all the names of Papago individuals mentioned are fictitious, because the characters presented here are composites.

Page xv　　The introductory quote is from Father Thomas Merton, *Raids on the Unspeakable* (New York: New Directions, 1964), p. 9.

THE DESERT SMELLS LIKE RAIN: AN OVERTURE

Page 3　　Jose Pancho's Mockingbird Speech is printed in full, in Papago English, in the excellent collection of Papago texts: Ruth M. Underhill, Donald M. Bahr, Baptisto Lopez, Jose Pancho, and David Lopez, *Rainhouse and Ocean: Speeches for the Papago Year* (Flagstaff: Museum of Northern Arizona Press, 1979), p. 33.

Page 5　　I thank Dennis Cornejo of the Arizona-Sonora Desert Museum for introducing me to the orgies of spadefoot toads (*Scaphiopus couchi* and *S. hammondi*) which occur with the first drenching rains of the summer. Cornejo and Clay May have been studying the accelerated breeding and development cycle of Avra Valley spadefoots for several summers.

Page 6   The quote from linguist Pilcher uses another orthography. See William M. Pilcher, "Some Comments on the Folk Taxonomy of the Papago," *American Anthropologist* 69:2 (1967), 204–08.

Page 7   Ecologist Tevis published several articles on desert wildflowers which emphasize their remarkable responses to scanty rain. See Lloyd Tevis, Jr., "A Population of Desert Ephemerals Germinated by Less than One Inch of Rain," and "Germination and Growth of Ephemerals Induced by Sprinkling a Sandy Desert," *Ecology* 39:4 (1958), 688–95 and 681–88, respectively.

Page 8   Gary Nabhan, James Berry, Cynthia Anson, and Charles Weber, "Papago Indian Floodwater Fields and Tepary Bean Protein Yields," *Ecology of Food and Nutrition* 10:1 (1981), 71–78.

CHAPTER ONE: ON THE TRAIL OF I'ITOI

Page 13   The song dreamed by the Papago shaman is printed in Ruth M. Underhill, *Singing for Power: The Song Magic of the Papago Indians* (Berkeley: University of California Press, 1938), p. 144.

Page 13   The caracara, *Caracara cheriway*, is called *kusijim* by the Papago, and is recognized for the dark top of its head, and its feeding on roadkills. Pesticide buildup through the food chain has severely affected carrion-eaters which feed around modern agriculture in the Southwest, while those which spend most of their time in areas of traditional agriculture have hardly been affected. (Amadeo Rea, personal communication.)

Page 14   The various attributes of *I'itoi* have been summarized by Ruth Underhill, *Papago Indian Religion* (New York: Columbia University Press, 1946), p. 12.

Page 14   Non-Papago need permits to drive within the southern (border-land) districts of the Papago Indian Reservation.

Page 15   I thank Janice Bowers for helping identify the rare or unusually distributed plants found in Baboquivari Canyon. Their scientific names are noted below, since the plants are rare enough in the U.S. that their English common names are not generally used: kidneywood, *Eysenhardtia polystachya*; Arizona sapote, *Bumelia lanuginosa*; white-flowered plumbago, *Plumbago scandens*; bloodleaf amaranth, *Iresine heterophylla*; wild chiles or chiltepines, *Capsicum annuum*; desert dogbane, *Amsonia kear-*

neyana; and elephant tree, *Bursera fagaroides*. The five-striped sparrow, *Aimophila quinquestriata*, nests in few places in the U.S. (Baboquivari Canyon, Sonoita Creek) (Scott Mills, personal communication). Coatimundis of the borderlands are the subject of a delightful book by Bil Gilbert, *Chulo* (New York: Knopf, 1973). A sizable portion of the book discusses Kitt Peak *changos*, pp. 74–118.

Page 16   I have discussed the Papago wild chile harvest in Gary Paul Nabhan, "Chiltepines: Wild Spice of the American Southwest," *El Palacio* 84:2 (1978), 1–5. The wild onions, called *I'itoi siwol* by the Papago, likely include more than one *Allium* species. An edible root, whose Papago name is *ṣa:ḍ*, is known to some as saiya or wild carrot; its scientific name is *Amoreuxia palmatifida*.

Page 17   The story of the overstuffed mouse is found in Underhill, *Papago Indian Religion*, p. 11.

Page 19   A number of more common species of the Arizona Uplands of the Sonoran Desert are found in the canyon. Their common names follow J. Harry Lehr, *A Catalogue of the Flora of Arizona* (Phoenix: Desert Botanical Garden, 1978).

Page 19   The definition and story of *Waw Kiwulik* as "rock drawn in the middle" is from the Papago myths collected by Harold Bell Wright, *Long Ago Told* (New York: Appleton, 1979), pp. 135–40. Kino's transcription is noted by Herbert Eugene Bolton, *Rim of Christendom* (New York: Macmillan, 1936), p. 399.

Page 20   Observations on the geology and history of *I'itoi ki:* were written by Robert H. Forbes, "Notes on the Baboquivaris," July 26, 1948, a three-page memo deposited in the Arizona Historical Society archives. Dr. Forbes, a famous scientist and conservationist, was the first man known to climb Baboquivari Peak. When one Papago saw Forbes' campfire atop the Peak, he cried to his village that the world was coming to an end.

CHAPTER TWO: THROWING UP THE CLOUDS

Page 25   The chapter's introductory quote was transcribed by Underhill, *Papago Indian Religion*, p. 57.

Page 25   Excerpts from this chapter appeared in the saguaro ethnobotany literature review done by Frank S. Crosswhite, "The Annual Saguaro Harvest and Crop Cycle of the Papago, with Reference to Ecology and Symbolism," *Desert Plants* 2:1 (1980), 1–62. Dr.

Crosswhite's article skillfully weaves together many references to the Papago wine feast, providing many new insights.

Page 26   See Pilcher, "Some Comments on the Folk Taxonomy of the Papago," 205.

Page 26   The legend of the saguaro and Crow (White-necked Raven) is found in Underhill, *Papago Indian Religion*, p. 42.

Page 31   The best technical study of the ecology of Papago saguaro harvesting is by William H. Doelle, "Desert resources and Hohokam subsistence: the Conoco-Florence project," *Arizona State Museum Archaeological Series* 103 (1977), 70–77; 94–99.

Page 31   The 1929 price of saguaro syrup is noted in a valuable early article by Frank A. Thackery and A. R. Leding, "The Giant Cactus of Arizona: The Use of Its Fruit and Other Cactus Fruits by the Indians," *Journal of Heredity* 20:9 (1929), 400–14.

Page 31   Papago in villages north of the U.S./Mexico border used to migrate southward to take advantage of denser stands of organ pipe, *Stenocereus thurberi*, and to sell surplus fruit to Mexicans. (Henry Dobyns, personal communication.)

Page 32   Attempts to make the wine feasts illegal are discussed in Crosswhite, "The Annual Saguaro Harvest," 54.

Page 33   Underhill et al. (1979) provide texts from Santa Rosa wine feast orations, pp. 25–30, 32–35. I attended the wine drinking in 1978, 1979, and 1980, as well as one night of dancing in 1979. These ceremonies were held by the people of two related villages and occurred much later in the season (as late as August 31) than most dates reported in the historic literature. This suggests that the ceremony now functions not so much to initiate the rains, but to continue them, as well as to reaffirm the Papago heritage.

Page 36   Andrew Weil, "Throwing Up in Mexico," *The Marriage of the Sun and Moon, A Quest for Unity in Consciousness* (Boston: Houghton Mifflin, 1970), chapter 2.

Page 36   Underhill, *Papago Indian Religion*, p. 67.

Page 36   Crosswhite, p. 40–43, suggests that the saguaro wine-making process may have recently shifted from yeast to acetic fermentation, which would make the fruit turn to wine then to vinegar in a short period of time. This is doubtful.

Page 36   Andrew Weil, pp. 10–12.

Page 37   The account of the Franciscan father Garcés observing a 1776 Pima wine feast is found in *On the Trail of a Spanish Pioneer*, ed.

Elliott Coues (New York: Francis P. Harper, 1900), 2, 438–40. Dr. Henry Dobyns graciously corrected and amended Coues' translation, using the original Spanish as written by Garces, *Diario de exploraciones en Arizona y California en los años de 1775 y 1776* (Mexico: UNAM/IIH, 1968), 6, 87.

CHAPTER THREE: WHAT DO YOU DO WHEN THE RAIN IS DYING?

Page 41   The chapter's introductory quote is from Juan Smith's version of the *O'odham* origin, as transcribed by Julian Hayden, "Pima Creation Myth" (Spring, 1935), 23. This rich oral history remains unpublished, in manuscript form, in the Arizona State Museum Archives.

Page 41   *Charco* is a Spanish loan word used here interchangeably with floodwater reservoir and/or runoff catchment pond. Historically, *charcos* were used as a source of drinking water; today they are used primarily for livestock watering, and secondarily as a source of water for irrigation.

Page 41   San Juan's Day, June 24, is the date which Sonoran Indians associate with the probable start of the summer rains. Many Papago and Mexican farmers believe the rains have diminished since the last century. Scientists have detected that heavy summer rains may be less frequent, and that there is a slight trend toward aridity in southern Arizona, but have recorded no significant changes in total rainfall. See Ronald Cooke and Richard W. Reeves, *Arroyos and Environmental Change in the American Southwest* (Oxford: Clarendon, 1976), p. 78.

Page 41   For background on Papago crops, see Edward F. Castetter and Willis H. Bell, *Pima and Papago Agriculture* (Albuquerque: University of New Mexico Press, 1942). Since this publication was issued, numerous studies have confirmed that Papago crops have both physiological and morphological adaptations to heat and drought over and above conventional crop varieties. See Nabhan et al., "Papago Indian Floodwater Fields and Tepary Bean Protein Yields," *The Kiva* (1979). See also Edgar Anderson, "Maize in the Southwest," *Landscape Papers* (Berkeley: Turtle Island Foundation, 1976), chapter 7.

Page 42   Papago field weeds are listed in Gary Paul Nabhan, "The Ecology of Floodwater Farming in Southwestern North America," *Agro-Ecosystems 5* (1979), 245–55. Many of these weeds are useful plants and occur in greater abundance in the fields than in any other desert habitat. I was one of the many contributors to the pamphlet on Papago greens prepared by Meals for Millions and Save the Children: *O'odham I:wakĭ: Wild Greens of the Desert People* (Tucson: MFM/Southwest, 1980).

Page 43　For more on *O'odham* hunting in fields, there are two excellent articles: Amadeo M. Rea, "The Ecology of Pima Fields," *Environment Southwest* 484 (1979), 1–6; and "Hunting Lexemic Categories of the Pima Indians," *The Kiva* 44:2–3 (1979), 113–19. Dr. Rea suggests that birds and mammals were attracted to the greater availability of food and shelter in fields, and that specialized forms of hunting developed to take advantage of their presence.

Page 46　Charles Bowden, *Killing the Hidden Waters* (Austin: University of Texas Press, 1977). This book is perhaps the most evocative vision of the historic Papago relationship to water, and a key text on groundwater problems as well.

Page 46　Enrique Campos-Lopez discussed his ideas on dry-land and run-off agriculture efficiency with reporter Mohan Ran, "Three Ways to Use Biomass for Energy," *Christian Science Monitor*, February 28, 1979, 17.

Page 46　Henry Dobyns, *Papagos in the Cotton Fields, 1950* (Tucson: Dobyns, 1951), available in the Arizona State Museum Archives. As commercial cotton growing developed in Arizona, Papago left their own fields to do wage work. Mechanization later replaced them, but their fields were already overgrown.

Page 47　I have discussed the historic abandonment of desert-adapted crops in several articles, including: Gary P. Nabhan and Richard S. Felger, "Teparies in Southwestern North America," *Economic Botany* 32:1 (1978), 2–19; Gary Paul Nabhan, "Seeds of Prehistory," *Garden* 4:3 (1980), 8–12.

Page 47　Daniel H. Janzen, "The Deflowering of Central America," *Natural History* 83:4 (1974), 49. Janzen was referring to the extinction of relationships between pollinators and wild plants, but his concept applies to other long-evolved ecological interactions as well.

Page 47　The acreage figures are derived from several sources, and discussed in Nabhan et al., "Legumes in the O'odham Diet," *The Kiva* (1979).

Page 47　For evidence of the beneficial effects of wild *Amaranthus* on corn pests, see Miguel A. Altieri and W. H. Whitcomb, "The Potential

Use of Weeds in the Manipulation of Beneficial Insects," *Hort-Science* 14:1 (1979), 12–18.

Page 47 Bean ecologist Russell Buhrow and I discovered naturally occurring *Rhizobia* nodules on month-old tepary bean roots in a small Papago field. It is possible that the nitrogen-fixing bacteria washed into the field from nearby wild tepary populations. Scientists have seldom had luck getting *Rhizobia* established on beans in the desert. See Gary Nabhan, Ken Vogler, and Karen Reichhardt, "Tepary Bean Crop Ecology, Papago Indian Reservation, Arizona," *Bean Improvement Cooperative Newsletter* (1981).

Page 47 The bee, *Perdita hurdi*, has been found on perennial *Proboscidea* flowers, but it was reported that investigators searched in vain for it in wild *Proboscidea parviflora* populations. See Paul D. Hurd, Jr., and E. Gordon Linsley, "Pollination of the Unicorn Plant (Martyniaceae) by an Oligolectic Corolla-Cutting Bee (Hymenoptera: Apoidea)," *Journal of the Kansas Entomological Society* 36:4 (1963), 348–52. Subsequently, I found *Perdita hurdi* in a large patch of domesticated annual devil's claw *(Proboscidea parviflora)*, where a large flower population may have been providing the bees with "rewards" analogous to those of the perennial species.

CHAPTER FOUR: CHANGOS DEL DESIERTO

Page 51 Celestine Pablo wrote the introductory story for me when I taught creative natural history writing on the reservation through the Arizona Writers on the Road Program. I thank the Papago children who wrote such wonderful stories for me, including Carman Martin, who is also quoted. I also wish to express gratitude to Shelly Cohn of the Arizona Commission of Arts and Humanities for coordinating my participation in the program.

Page 52 Timothy Garcia's story was also written during my Writers on the Road classes. It was published in a special folio of Indian children's writing and drawings in *Suntracks* 3:2 (1980), 24. I thank Larry Evers and the board of Indian students who showed interest in these stories.

Page 52 The *Ne:big* is the most widely known of these mythical creatures. A fine translation of a *Ne:big* story, as well as the original Papago text, is found in Dean and Lucille Saxton, *O'odham Hoho'ok A'agitha—Legends and Lore of the Papago and Pima Indians* (Tucson: University of Arizona Press, 1973), pp. 305–16.

Page 53   The story of the search for the Badger boy is a composite of several tales, including one highlighted by Stanley Throssell, "Searchers Rescue Cobabi Boy, 2½," *Papago Runner* 1:14 (1977), 1.

Page 55   I thank Papago police officer Ed Noriego for taking time to relate several personal experiences searching for children lost in the desert.

Page 56   For a classic discussion of dehydration, see K. Schmidt-Nielson, *Desert Animals* (London: Oxford University Press, 1954).

Page 58   Certain elderly Papago have an aversion to being photographed. They believe that a photo captures a person's soul, causing the person to die sooner.

Page 60   The locoweed (*Astragalus*) pods are called *gopsikud*, and are stomped on to make "bang" at fiestas.

Page 61   The Children's Shrine story has many beautiful versions, each with a slightly different descriptive and philosophical emphasis. The one presented here is largely from what I have been told directly by Papago, but is influenced by two recordings: Saxton and Saxton, *O'odham Hoho'ok A'agitha*, pp. 341–46; and Underhill, *Papago Indian Religion*, pp. 68–69.

CHAPTER FIVE: RAISING HELL AS WELL AS WHEAT

Page 67   The introductory quote of this chapter is from an article in *El Imparcial*, the newspaper of Hermosillo, Sonora, Mexico, date and page unknown. The quote was shown to me by Rafael Alfonso Garcia V., Gobernador General del Tribu Pápago en Sonora. I thank the several Sonoran Papago who discussed this sensitive issue with me. See also Bernard L. Fontana, *Of Earth and Little Rain* (Flagstaff: Northland Press, 1981), pp. 75–78.

Page 67   This chapter appeared in another form in *La Confluencia—A Magazine of the Southwest* 3:3–4 (1980), 18–22. Several clarifications have been made.

Page 68   Much of the history of Papago and Pima reaction to the Gadsden Purchase is summarized in the classic study, Edward H. Spicer, *Cycles of Conquest* (Tucson: University of Arizona, 1962), pp. 133–47.

Page 72   Several articles by Mr. and Mrs. Stanley Throssell provide the best coverage of U.S. Papago responses to the Sonoran Papago problem. See "Sonoran Papagos Recognized," *The Papago Runner* 3:8 (1979), 5; and "Sonoran Papagos Press for Land and Recognition," and "To Get Their Land Perseverance Is Needed," *The Papago Runner* 3:11 (1979), 1. The U.S. tribe is still working to decide the wisest ways to utilize the $26 million land claims reward. It may not necessarily use part of these funds for this problem, but has helped Sonoran Papago through its existing programs.

Page 74   *Colonistas* are typically those Mexicans from further south who Sonorans perceive as migrating north to take advantage of less-populated lands in Sonora. There is increasing tension between native Sonoran families, who feel their land is being usurped, and those from other areas in Mexico who are forced to seek new opportunities because of population pressure. For balanced accounts of demographic change affecting the borderlands, see Paul R. Ehrlich, Loy Bilderback, and Ann H. Ehrlich, *The Golden Door—International Migration, Mexico and the United States* (New York: Ballantine Books, 1979), pp. 92–275; and Tom Miller, *On the Border* (New York: Harper and Row, 1981), pp. 178–79.

Page 74   San Isidro is patron saint of agriculture for Papago and other Catholics; he is revered as an intermediary who can help bring rains for plantings. Often, farmers put pictures of this *santo* out in their fields before the rains come, to help initiate them.

CHAPTER SIX: PLANTS WHICH COYOTE STEALS

Page 77   The most readable collection of Coyote stories are reworked legends from various tribes: Barry Holstun Lopez, *Giving Birth to Thunder, Sleeping With His Daughter, Coyote Builds North America* (New York: Avon, 1981). Nothing, on the other hand, beats a Coyote legend told by a well-versed Indian storyteller with all the timing, inflection, and gestures that print can never capture.

Page 77   The story of Coyote making malformed people has many versions. For a comparison of various versions, see Donald M. Bahr, "On the Complexity of Southwest Indian Emergence Myths," *Journal of Anthropological Research* 33:3 (1977), 317–48.

Page 77   A similar story, with carrying positions reversed, appears in Frank Russell, *The Pima Indians*, edited by Bernard L. Fontana (Tucson: University of Arizona Press, 1975), p. 217.

Page 79   See Madeline Mathiot, *A Dictionary of Papago Usage*, Language Science Monographs 8:2 (Bloomington: Indiana University Publications, 1973), p. 144. Mathiot lists *ban vuhioṣa* as a hoe, but this term is generally used by Papago for pick-axe and/or a Pulaski.

Page 79   A:ḍ is not to be confused with another wild gourd, aḍawĭ, the finger gourd, *Cucurbita digitata*. Most Northern Pimans use *a:ḍ* for *Apodanthera*, because *Cucerbita foetidissima* occurs mostly at higher elevations. Some may know all three wild cucurbits, and it should be interesting to see which names they use. See W. P. Bemis and Thomas W. Whitaker, "The Xerophytic *Cucurbita* of Northwestern Mexico and Southwestern United States," *Madrano* 20:2 (1969); Gary Nabhan, "Ethnobotany of Wild Cucurbits in Arid North America—An Annotated Bibliography" (unpublished manuscript, Tucson, University of Arizona College of Agriculture, 1972).

Page 80   For background on squash domestication, see Thomas W. Whitaker and W. P. Bemis, "Origin and Evolution of Cultivated Cucurbita," *Bulletin of the Torrey Botanical Club* 102:106 (1975), 362–68.

Page 80   *Ban Tokĭ* is *Gossypium thurberi*, the wild cotton species common in southern Arizona canyons. It is sometimes a protected weed in Papago fields.

Page 81   *Ban Bawĭ* is *Phaseolus acutifolius* var. *latifolius*, also common in Sonoran Desert canyons. It is discussed in Gary P. Nabhan, Charles W. Weber, and James W. Berry, "Legumes in the Papago-Pima Indian Diet and Ecological Niche," *The Kiva* 44:2–3 (1979), 173–90.

Page 81   I have collaborated on studies on the relationship between wild and domesticated *Proboscidea* with several scientists, yet most of the folk taxonomy and ethnographic knowledge remains unpublished. *Ban Ṣu:sk* is *Proboscidea althaefolia*, and *I'hug* is domesticated *P. parviflora*. The wild *P. parviflora* can be either *I'hug* or *Ban I'hug-ga*, but the latter term is used for *P. altheaefolia* as well. For more on the botanical aspects, see Gary Nabhan, Alfred Whiting, Henry Dobyns, Richard Hevly, and Robert Euler, "Devil's Claw Domestication: Evidence from Southwestern Indian Fields," *Journal of Ethnobiology* 1:1 (1981), 135–64.

Page 83   The story of Coyote's tobacco collected by Juan Dolores is transcribed in Papago in Saxton and Saxton, *O'othham Hoho'ok A'agitha*, 42–44, and paraphrased into English by them. The version included here is my own paraphrase or loose translation.

Page 84   The second Coyote's tobacco story is derived from Underhill, *Papago Indian Religion*, 83–85; and from a version told by River Pima storyteller Joseph Giff. A videotaping of his complete version was made by the Tucson Public Library. I thank the library staff for providing me with a transcript of it.

Page 84   See Jack R. Harlan, "Genetic Resources in Wild Relatives of Crops," *Crop Science* 16 (1976), 329–33.

Page 85   The triple hybrid which includes wild *Gossypium thurberi* was first made by J. O. Beasley; it is discussed by Thomas Kerr, "Transference of Lint Length into Upland Cotton," *Proceedings of the Cotton Improvement Conference* 3 (1951).

Page 85   Dr. Hiroshi Muramoto of the University of Arizona is currently attempting to transfer the narrow, caudal bract character of wild cotton species to cultivated cottons.

Page 85   See Shigemi Honma, "Bean Interspecific Hybrid," *Journal of Heredity* 41 (1956), 247–52; and Howard Scott Gentry, "Origin of the Common Bean, *Phaseolus vulgaris,*" *Economic Botany* 23:1 (1969), 55–69. The progress of Dr. Giles Waines and Claire Thomas in using wild teparies for bean improvement can be followed in forthcoming issues of the *Bean Improvement Cooperative Newsletter.*

Page 86   For a discussion of the usefulness of wild cucurbits, and their disease resistance, see Thomas W. Whitaker and Robert J. Knight, Jr., "Collecting Cultivated and Wild Cucurbits in Mexico," *Economic Botany* 34:4 (1980), 309–11.

CHAPTER SEVEN: WHERE THE BIRDS ARE OUR FRIENDS

Page 89   The introductory quote is from Ronald L. Ives, "The Monster of Quitovac," *Masterkey* 15 (1941), 196–98. Ives tried too hard to find what the Monster was, suggesting it to be a representation of now extinct Pleistocene megafauna that Papago oral history "remembered." From other versions, e.g., Saxton and Saxton, *O'othham Hoho'ok A'agitha,* p. 305, the *Ne:big* is obviously allegorical: it "just lay there and could draw people to it with its breath." *Ki:towak* equals Quitovac.

Page 89   For historic names, see Wilton H. Hoy, "A Quest for the Meaning of Quitobaquito," *The Kiva* 34:4 (1969), 213–18.

Page 90   Carl Lumholtz, *New Trails in Mexico* (New York: Scribner's, 1912), p. 286.

Page 91   Sandfood, or *Pholisma sonorae,* is known to Papago as *hia taḍk.* See Gary Nabhan, "*Ammobroma sonorae,* an Endangered Parasitic Plant in Extremely Arid North America," *Desert Plants* 2:3 (1980), 188–96.

Page 91   R. Jones, "The Wi'igita of Achi and Quitobac," *The Kiva* 36:4 (1971), 1–29.

Page 93   Hoy's "A Quest for the Meaning of Quitobaquito" does mention tules as part of the meaning of the word, but also mentions a dozen other permutations. When asked what *Ki:towak* means, residents there simply pull up a tule, *Scirpus olneyi*, which they call *wak*, and which relates to the origin myth of the oasis.

Page 93   The fencerows planted are similar to those described in Amadeo Rea, "The Ecology of Pima Fields."

Page 93   The plants of Quitobaquito are included in Janice Bowers, "Flora of Organ Pipe Cactus National Monument," *Journal of the Arizona Nevada Academy of Science* 15:1–2 (1980). I have been working on a flora of *Ki:towak*, which already amounts to seventy-two plant species, including numerous species not at Quitobaquito. The so-called endangered Quitobaquito endemic aster, *Machaeranthera arizonica*, occurs in houseyards and fields at *Ki:towak*.

Page 94   Ronald L. Ives, "Some Papago migrations in the Sonoyta Valley," *Masterkey* 10 (1936), 161–67.

Page 94   The archaeology of the area is summarized by Lynn S. Teague, "Letter Report Re: Archaeological Survey and Mapping, Quitobaquito Springs, Organ Pipe National Monument," November 30, 1977, on file at the Arizona State Museum.

Page 94   See Tom Childs, "History of Quitobaquito," an updated one-page summary noting residents since the 1930s, on file at Organ Pipe Cactus National Monument. Since Childs lived there and married into the Papago family dwelling there, it is an important document.

Page 94   According to a July 29, 1979, letter to me from Park Service historian Bill Hoy, Jim Orosco received $13,000 for "squatter's rights" in Organ Pipe, including six-and-one-half acres of cultivated land and 24,699.22 acres that had been used for grazing or other purposes by Papago. I thank Mr. Hoy, the most diligent historian of Organ Pipe.

Page 95   Descendants of Juan José now living in Manager's Dam are among those who tell the story of *S-Iawuis Wo:da*. Since it is not known if there were any verbal agreements between Jim Orosco and other Papago at the time, it is still unclear whether he was acting "on behalf" of other descendants of Juan José and José Juan. Ethnohistorian Jack Forbes has argued that legally, "Indian title" should hold for any land that the Papago as a group have used for religious purposes, as guaranteed by an 1853 treaty. See Jack D. Forbes, *The Papago-Apache Treaty of 1853* (Davis: University of California Native American Studies Tecumseh Center, 1979), p. 27.

Page 95　Bob Thomas, "Price of Progress Comes High," *Arizona Republic* (Sunday, August 6, 1967), Section 18:A.

Page 96　I visited *Ki:towak* and Quitobaquito in different seasons in collaboration with ornithologists: December 1979 (Peter Warshall); May 1979 (Brian Brown); September 1980 (Amadeo Rea). A cumulative list of birds seen at Quitobaquito over the years is on file at Organ Pipe. I have detailed bird and plant lists from *Ki:towak* and *A'al Waipia* on file, and will share them with any interested scientist.

CHAPTER EIGHT: GATHERING

Page 101　The introductory quote is in Ruth Underhill, *Autobiography of a Papago Woman* (Menasha, Wis.: American Anthropological Association, 1936), republished augmented edition (New York: Holt, Rinehart, Winston, 1979).

Page 101　*Pimería Alta* is a term referring to northern Sonoran Desert lands historically inhabited by Papago and River Pima populations. Much of the disease data for this chapter was gathered by researchers working with River Pima patients, but the same syndromes occur among nearly all the Papago.

Page 101　Kelly M. West, "Diabetes in American Indians and Other Native Populations of the New World," *Diabetes* 23:10 (1974), 841. For information on the high incidence of diabetes (now at least fifty-five percent among adult Papago), see William C. Knowler, Peter H. Bennett, Richard F. Hamman, and Max Miller, "Diabetes Incidence and Prevalence in Pima Indians: A 19-Fold Greater Incidence Than in Rochester, Minnesota," *American Journal of Epidemiology* 108:6 (1978), 497–505.

Page 101　Charles R. Strotz and Gregory I. Shorr, "Hypertension in the Papago Indians," *Circulation* 48 (1973), 1299–1303.

Page 101　M. Pijoan, C. A. Elkin, and C. O. Elsinger, "Ascorbic Acid Deficiency Among Papago Indians," *Journal of Nutrition* 25 (1944), 491–96; Katherine Cleft, "A Comparison of Nutritional Deficiencies Among School Children on the Papago Reservation in 1954 and 1965" (unpublished manuscript, Casa Grande, 1965), p. 7.

Page 102　Although reducing caloric consumption can help diabetics, evidence is accumulating that the metabolic rate of the obese may reinforce their condition, with more weight gained per volume of calories consumed. See for instance the anonymous note on the work of Dr. Roger Unger, Dr. Peter Bennett, and Dr. Ethan Sims, "Diabetes Research Focuses on Desert Tribe," *Research Resources Reporter* s.n. (May 1979), 6.

Page 102 Jeanne M. Reid, et al., "Nutrient Intake of Pima Indian Women: Relationships to Diabetes Mellitus and Gall Bladder Disease," *American Journal of Clinical Nutrition* 24 (1971), 1281–89.

Page 103 A site near Pinacate Peak cultivated by Sand Papago near the turn of the century may have been among the most arid localities in the world where agriculture has been practiced. See Carl Lumholtz, *New Trails in Mexico*, p. 217.

Page 105 The concept of abundant nutritional resources in the desert has been advanced primarily by Dr. Richard Felger. See R. S. Felger and M. B. Moser, "Seri Indian Food Plants: Desert Subsistence Without Agriculture," *Ecology of Food and Nutrition* 5 (1976), 13–17; and R. S. Felger and G. P. Nabhan, "Deceptive Barrenness," *Ceres* 9:2 (1976), 34–39.

Page 105 For an extensive list of major *O'odham* plant and animal foods, see Bernard L. Fontana, "Man in Arid Lands—the Pima Indians of the Sonoran Desert," *Desert Biology* 2 (New York: Academic Press, 1974), 489–528.

Page 105 On protein quality of Papago foods, see G. P. Nabhan, C. W. Weber, and. W. Berry, *The Kiva* 44:2–3, 175.

Page 106 Sections of the excellent thesis by Ruth Greenhouse on mineral content in Pima foods are being prepared for journal articles. In the meantime, consult Ruth Greenhouse, "The Iron and Calcium Content of Some Traditional Pima Foods and the Effect of Preparation Methods" (Tempe: Arizona State University, 1979). See also M. Pijoan, et al., *Journal of Nutrition* 25, for vitamin values.

Page 106 Discussion of the greens and their seasonality is in Meals for Millions, *O'odham I:wakĭ*, pp. 1–3.

Page 106 *Waik Wiyo:di* or "Three Acorns" is a valley near Arivaca where Papago, Apache, and Mexican families regularly go to collect the non-bitter acorns of *Quercus emoryi*.

Page 108 D. H. Calloway, R. D. Giaque, and F. M. Costa, "The Superior Mineral Content of Some American Indian Foods in Comparison to Federally Donated Counterpart Commodities," *Ecology of Food and Nutrition* 3 (1974), 203–12. Calloway's colleague, Dr. Harriet

Kuhnlein, has extended this nutritional ethnobotanical research into many new areas. For instance, she recently found indigenous salts and plant ash consumed by native Americans to be higher in essential trace elements than either refined (table) salt or health store sea salts. See Harriet V. Kuhnlein, "The Trace Element Content of Indigenous Salts Compared with Commercially Refined Substitutes," *Ecology of Food and Nutrition* 10 (1981), 113–21.

Page 108   Peter H. Bennett, "The Pima Indians: Do They Hold the Key?" *Diabetes Forecast* (July-August 1977), 22–24.

Page 109   The direct quotes from Peter Bennett and Roger Unger appeared in the anonymous interview in *Research Resources Reporter* (May 1979), 6.

Page 110   On prickly pear pads as a therapeutic food for diabetics, see Ruben Roman Ramos, "Una observación clínica sobre el efecto hipoglucemente del nopal (*Opuntia* sp.)," *Medicina Tradicional* 3:10 (1980), 9–11.

CHAPTER NINE: GIVEN OVER TO SANTOS AND SPICES

Page 113   The introductory quote is an excerpt from my poem, "Chasing Magdalena," which first appeared in *The Blue Cloud Quarterly* 22:4 (1976), unnumbered.

Page 113   This chapter was written upon the suggestion of Dr. Henry Dobyns, whose ethnohistoric and ethnographic studies of the Magdalena Fiesta over three decades are unsurpassed by any other study of Sonoran Desert fiestas. This description of Papago at the fiesta is dedicated to Dr. Dobyns and his wife, Mary Faith.

Page 113   See George H. Williamson, "Why the Pilgrims Come," *The Kiva* 16:1–2 (1950), 2–7; and Henry F. Dobyns, "Magdalena Festival," *Sonoran Heritage Play Leaming Packet* (Tucson: Tucson Public Library, 1979), 1–11. These essays relate how St. Francis temporarily disappeared from Magdalena in the 1930s, when an anti-clerical movement in Mexico attempted to terminate the fiesta and veneration of the statue. The St. Francis figure is said to have burrowed into the ground near the tiny Papago village of *Cuwĭ Gu:ṣk*, Sonora, now known as San Francisquito. The holy figure was stumbled upon by a Papago, who took it into his village's chapel. Since that time, many western Papago trek to *Cuwĭ Gu:ṣk* rather than to Magdalena, claiming that this tiny village still maintains the original St. Francis. The discovery was interpreted by many Catholics to mean that St. Francis was indestructible. The pilgrimage to San Francisquito continues. In 1980, a mini-fiesta was held on October 3 and 4, which included a Papago *waila* band with electric instruments.

Page 114   See George B. Eckhart and James S. Griffith, *Temples in the Wilderness* (Tucson: Arizona Historical Society, 1975), p. 27.

Page 115   See Agustin A. Zamora, *La Cohetera, Mi Barrio* (Mexico, D.F.: Estado de Sonora, 1944), p. 104. Dr. Margarita Kay translated this quote.

Page 115   Elisabeth Tooker, "The Pilgrims in Church," *The Kiva* 16:1–2 (1950), 9–13.

Page 116   Dobyns, *Magdalena Festival*, p. 4.

Page 116   For a perspective on early long-distance trade, see Carrol L. Riley, "Mesoamerican Indians in the Early Southwest," *Ethnohistory* 21 (1974), 25–26.

Page 117   Evidence of Papago being involved in historic trade of plants and animals beyond their natural ranges is well-documented for chiles in Castetter and Bell, *Pima and Papago Indian Agriculture*, p. 121; and for macaws in Rufus K. Wyllys, "Padre Luis Velarde's Relation of Pimeria Alta, 1716," *New Mexico Historical Review* 6 (1931), 111–57.

Page 117   Dobyns, *Magdalena Festival*, p. 5.

Page 117   Margarita Artschwager Kay, "Health and Illness in a Mexican American Barrio," *Ethnic Medicine in the Southwest*, ed. Edward Spicer (Tucson: University of Arizona, 1977), p. 122.

Page 117   Background on the history of commonly used Southwestern herbs can be obtained from Margarita Artschwager Kay, "The *Florilegio Medicinal*: Source of Southwest Medicine," *Ethnohistory* 24:3 (1977), 251–59. For several herbs, the chemical constituents and physiologically active properties are known. See Edward S. Ayensu, "Plants for Medicinal Uses with Special Reference to Arid Zones," *Arid Lands Plant Resources*, ed. J. R. Goodin and David K. Northington (Lubbock: International Center for Arid and Semi-Arid Land Studies, Texas Tech University, 1979), pp. 117–78.

Page 117   The Sonoran Spanish names for the herbs are given in the text. They correspond to the following *O'odham* names (and scientific taxa): cocolmeca is *ṣa'i bawi (Phaseolus metcalfei* and *P. ritensis)*; jojoba is *hohowai (Simmondsia chinensis)*; yerba colorada is *wakwandam (Rumex hymenosephalus* or *Rumex crispus)*; yerba del manzo is *wa:wisa* (*Anemopsis californica*); hediondilla is *ṣegai* (*Larrea tridentata*); *cucupa:di* is *Liguisticum porteri*; and wild chamomile is known to both Papago and mestizos as *manzanilla* (*Matricaria matricarioides*). These plants are described in the Pima ethnobotany by L. S. M. Curtin, *By the Prophet of the Earth* (Santa Fe: San Vicente Foundation, 1949), and in G. P. Nabhan, J. W. Berry, and C. W. Weber, "Wild Beans of the Greater Southwest: *Phaseolus metcalfei* and *P. ritensis*," *Economic Botany* 34:1 (1980), 68–85. Dr. Amadeo Rea and I have verified their identifications with voucher specimens. Spanish has been the *lingua franca* in the herb trade for 200 years, and some Papago do know the Spanish names for herbs.

CHAPTER TEN: YOU MAKE THE EARTH GOOD

Page 123   The introductory quote from Rosamund Spicer appears in Alice Joseph, Rosamund Spicer, and Jane Chesky, *The Desert People* (Chicago: University of Chicago Press, 1949), p. 39.

Page 123   This chapter was inspired by conversations with and an essay by Wendell Berry, "The Gift of Good Land—A Biblical Argument for Ecological Responsibility," *Sierra Club Bulletin* (November-December 1979), 20–26. I am also indebted to Cynthia Anson, who first alerted me to Papago soil taxonomy, sharing notes and collaborating on interviews of farmers with me.

Page 124   Papago soil renewal techniques and their efficacy will be discussed in detail in a work in progress. Runoff farming studies have concentrated on water-harvesting efficiencies while overlooking "nutrient-harvesting" in traditional fields.

Page 125   *Wako'ola* means something akin to "drift," including water-washed debris, or humus.

Page 127   To place the organic matter content of desert soils in perspective, see George W. Cox and Michael D. Atkins, *Agricultural Ecology* (San Francisco: W. H. Freeman, 1979). The discussion of field soil erosion losses also draws upon the work of Wes Jackson, *New Roots for Agriculture* (San Francisco: Friends of the Earth, 1980).

Page 128   E. M. Romney, A. Wallace, and R. B. Hunter, "Plant Response to Nitrogen Fertilization in the Northern Mohave Desert and Its Relation to Water Manipulation," in *Nitrogen in Desert Ecosystems*, N. E. West and J. Skukins, editors (Stroudsburg: Dowden, Hutchinson, and Ross, 1978), pp. 232–42.

Page 128   H. V. Clotts, "History of the Papago Indians and History of Irrigation, Papago Indian Reservations, Arizona" (unpublished manuscript, U.S. Indian Service, 1917).

Page 129   Gary Nabhan, "Indian Farmers Dive Into Arizona Water Battle,"
High Country News 9:6 (August 12, 1977), 7; and Tony Walther,
"Leasing Red Tape Ties Up Reservation Farming," *Pima-Maricopa
Echo* 6 (June 1980), 5–6 (reprinted from *Tri-Valley Dispatch*).

About the Author

Gary Paul Nabhan is an Arab American agro-ecologist, ethno-botanist, literary naturalist, and Ecumenical Franciscan Brother who lives near the U.S.-Mexico border. His collaborations with O'odham families and pueblos on both sides of the border now spans forty-five years. He is the recipient of a MacArthur Genius Award, a Labán Literary Fellowship, and several other honors for his cross-cultural, community-based conservation initiatives to safeguard and restore biocultural diversity, sacred places, and food traditions. He holds the W. K. Kellogg Chair in Borderlands Foods and Water Security at the University of Arizona Southwest Center.